The History of

WILLS EYE HOSPITAL

The History of

WILLS EYE HOSPITAL

WILLIAM TASMAN, M.D.

Co-Director, 'Retina Service, Wills Eye Hospital; Professor of Ophthalmology, Thomas Jefferson University, Philadelphia, Pennsylvania; Professor
and Director, Department of Ophthalmology, Medical College of Pennsylvania; Consultant, Children's Hospital; Attending Surgeon, Chestnut Hill
Hospital, Philadelphia

On the Occasion of the Dedication
of the third Wills Eye Hospital

April 1980

HARPER & ROW, PUBLISHERS

HAGERSTOWN

Cambridge		London
New York		Mexico City
Philadelphia		São Paulo
San Francisco		Sydney

1817

Library of Congress Cataloging in Publication Data

Tasman, William.
  The history of Wills Eye Hospital.

  "On the occasion of the dedication of third Wills Eye Hospital, April 1980."
  Include index.
  1. Hospitals, Ophthalmic and aural—Pennsylvania—Philadelphia—History.   2. Wills Hospital, Philadelphia.
I. Title.
RE3.P4T37   362.1′977′0974811   80-11180
ISBN 0-06-142531-1

To My Father
I. S. TASSMAN, M.D.
1892–1976
Attending Surgeon, Wills Eye Hospital
1939–1960

Contents

Preface

The purpose of this book is to present a concise, readable history of Wills Eye Hospital which can be easily digested in 1 to 2 hours. It is hoped that laymen as well as ophthalmologists will find it interesting and that they will be made aware of how colorful the history of Wills Eye Hospital has been. Some of the material is taken from the original *History of Wills Eye* published in 1931. Appropriate changes have been made and new chapters have been added to bring the history up to the present.

Many people have been helpful. To Dr. William Annesley goes the credit for suggesting the idea. Drs. Irving Leopold, Warren Reese, Francis Adler, and Owen Belmont and Mrs. Ruth Armour graciously supplied information. I would also like to thank the Pennsylvania Historical Society and Ms. Marion Solvay of the Athenaeum who assisted with the illustrations by Thomas Ustick Walter. I am also indebted to my wife, Alice Lea, for encouragement, and to my mother, Mrs. I. S. Tassman, who contributed mementos. Ms. Marilyn Fenichel and Dr. William Benson provided assistance, with the text, and Mrs. Mary Kennedy, Mrs. Mary Rafferty, and Ms. Cynthia Bolton typed and retyped the manuscript. Mr. David Silva prepared the illustrations, and Mr. Donald Beetem designed the cover.

Dr. Thomas Duane, our ophthalmologist-in-chief, and Mr. David Joseph, our administrator, were extremely supportive throughout.

Most of all, I am indebted to Dr. Harold Barnshaw, our Wills Eye historian, who loaned me his material and without whose help the book could not have been completed.

The assistance of Harper & Row, Publishers, in the publication of this book is gratefully acknowledged.

William Tasman, M.D.

The History of

WILLS EYE HOSPITAL

Chapter 1

The Founding of
Wills Eye Hospital

Many individuals have contributed to Wills Eye Hospital's reputation as one of the outstanding centers for eye care in the world. The funds necessary for growth and development were contributed by Philadelphia's leading philanthropists. Our staff not only has made countless advances in ophthalmology but also has been active in civic and cultural affairs. Indeed, many aspects of American history are reflected in the history of the Wills Eye Hospital.

Wills Eye Hospital owes its beginning to the Quaker tradition of charity. James Wills, Jr., founder of the hospital, was born in Philadelphia in 1777, just 1 year after the signing of the Declaration of Independence (Fig 1-1). His father, James Wills, Sr., had come to this country from England in 1748, probably to escape religious persecution. Details about the senior Wills' background are sketchy, but we do know that he was a member of the Philadelphia Monthly Meeting and for a time worked for Anthony Benezet. Benezet's family, French Huguenots, had been subjected to religious persecution in France and had fled to England, where they had joined the Society of Friends. Later, the family came to the United States, where Benezet immediately became active in programs to overcome racial prejudice. He established a school for blacks while teaching at the William Penn Charter School. Testimony to the love Benezet had for his fellowman was never more evident than at his funeral, when rich and poor alike gathered to honor this charitable man in one of the largest funerals ever to take place in the City of Brotherly Love.

Previous reports suggest that James Wills, Sr., probably worked for

1

Fig 1-1. The Graff House at 7th and Market Streets (four blocks from the new Wills) where Jefferson wrote the Declaration of Independence.

Benezet as his coachman. However, it is unlikely that Benezet ever had a coach, so this is doubtless erroneous (Fig 1-2). Nonetheless, Wills' friendship with Benezet probably had a great influence on Wills' later philanthropies, for which the money was earned in business. In 1791, with a stake of only $10, he opened his first store on Chestnut Street near Front Street.

On August 12, 1744, Wills married Hannah Roberts. The Roberts family was apparently quite well-to-do, and the newlyweds were

2

socially ostracized by the bride's friends because they suspected that she had married beneath her station. However, as it became obvious that Wills was a born businessman, he became accepted in the "proper" social circles.

Business prospered, and in 1800 Wills and his son, James, moved their store to 84 Chestnut Street (just above Third Street), which was, at that time, considered "West Philadelphia" (Fig 1-3). Shortly there-

Fig 1-2. Home of Anthony Benezet. (Courtesy of Pennsylvania Historical Society.)

THE

PHILADELPHIA

Directory and Register,

FOR 1821;

CONTAINING THE

NAMES, PROFESSIONS, AND RESIDENCE,

OF

All the Heads of Families

AND

PERSONS IN BUSINESS,

OF THE

City and Suburbs, Hamiltonville, and Camden, N. J.

WITH OTHER USEFUL INFORMATION.

━━━━━━━

PHILADELPHIA:

PUBLISHED BY M'CARTY & DAVIS,

No. 204, Market street.

....

1821.

Fig 1-3. The grocers of Chestnut Street were included in the Philadelphia Directory and Register.

Willits Phœbe, milliner 73 Arch
Willitts Archibald, carpenter, back 26 Cherry
Wills & Helverson, carpenters 106 Coates street
Wills James & Son, grocers 84 Chesnut
Wills James, jun. 84 Chesnut
†Wills John, labourer 154 Swanson
Wills Joseph, labourer 56 S. Second [*see Wells & Will*
Wills Josiah, cordwainer 81 Budd street

Fig 1-3. (*continued*).

after they purchased buildings on either side of No. 84 (82 and 86 Chestnut Street) (Figs 1-4 and 1-5).

Hannah Wills, James' mother, died between 1802 and 1809, and Wills Sr. died on April 23, 1823, at the age of 75. His obituary appeared in the paper on April 25.

Little is known about James Wills, Jr. He never married, and he continued his father's business until his premature death in 1823 at the young age of 48. No photographs of him exist. His death was sudden. His obituary appeared in *Poulson's American Daily Advertiser* on January 25, 1825 (Fig 1-6). James had added to his father's estate while spending little money on himself. His yearly expenses were estimated at $400, while his benefactions amounted to $1,500.

According to his will, which was dated May 5, 1823, and came to probate January 26, 1825, his estate at the time of his death was approximately $116,000 (Fig 1-7). With the exception of a few minor grants to places such as the Friends asylum for the insane and other worthwhile charities, the bulk of his wealth went to

the Mayor and Corporation of the City of Philadelphia for the time being and their successors in office forever, in trust for the purchase of sufficient plot of ground in the City of Philadelphia, or in the neighborhood thereof, and thereon to erect or cause to be erected suitable building and accommodations for a[n] hospital or asylum to be denominated—The Wills Hospital for the relief of the indigent, blind, and lame.

As so frequently happens, however, previously unheard-of heirs came forward to contest the will. Even in the 1800s, cases tended to drag on in the courts. It was not until March 21, 1831, that the Supreme Court of Pennsylvania finally decided in favor of the corporation of the city of Philadelphia, and the existence of the Wills Eye Hospital became assured.

Fig 1-4. Chestnut Street in the 1820s between Third and Fourth near Wills' grocery store. (Courtesy of Pennsylvania Historical Society.)

As it turns out, the delay was serendipitous: at the time of the bequest the sum available to establish a hospital was $108,395.35; however, in the interim, interest accrued, so that by the time work was ready to proceed on the hospital, funds available had risen to $122,548.57.

There has been much speculation about why James left his fortune as he did. One theory is that Wills became acquainted with Joseph Parrish, also a Quaker and one of the leading physicians and most prominent citizens in Philadelphia. Parrish would have known about the importance of establishing such an institution and no doubt would have transmitted his feelings to James. Further evidence of Parrish's influence over James is that all the other legacies left by Wills Jr. were to charities of particular interest to Parrish. In 1812, a sum of $5,000 went to the Friends asylum in Frankford, where Parrish served as one of the first attending physicians.

The City Council selected a plot between Eighteenth and Nineteenth Streets and between Race (then known as Sassafras) and Vine Streets, facing Logan Circle, for the new hospital. The cost of the ground was $20,000, not quite as good a deal as Peter Minuit's $24 buy of Manhattan Island, but considerably less than the more than $1 million the ground was worth in 1930 and a mere fraction of what that block commands today. Cost of the building was estimated at $57,203.69, which left a balance of $64,344.88. All in all, even taking into account the inflation over the years, the cost was significantly lower than that of the new Wills Eye Hospital—over $26 million.

Fig 1-5. Parade at the southeast corner of Fourth and Chestnut in the 1820s. (Courtesy of Pennsylvania Historical Society.)

Poulson's American Daily Advertiser

VOLUME LIV.]   TUESDAY MORNING, JANUARY 25, 1825.   [NUMBER 15,027.

OBITUARY.

DIED, suddenly, on the evening of the 22d. inst. JAMES WILLS, Grocer, in the 48th. year of his age.

His friends are respectfully invited to attend the burial, from his late residence, No. 84 Chesnut-street, this afternoon, at half past two o'clock.

Fig 1-6. Obituary of James Wills, Jr., as it appeared in *Poulson's American Daily Advertiser* on January 25, 1825. This is all we know about the sudden death of James Wills, Jr. Cause of death and, indeed, his style of living and even his appearance remain mysteries forever.

Logan Square, one of the four original squares laid out by William Penn and the site of the first Wills Eye Hospital, was named in honor of James Logan, William Penn's secretary, by an act of City Council in 1825. All of these four squares were originally set aside as open spaces for air, a designation similar to that made for the land upon which Moorfields Eye Hospital in London is built.

At that time, streets west of Broad Street were not paved and it was common to see cattle pasturing on nearby lands. Logan Square was also the site of a public hanging in 1823. A map of Philadelphia from 1840 shows that the Wills Eye Hospital was the only building built upon the ground bounding that square. The Cathedral of Saints Peter and Paul at the corner of Eighteenth and Race Streets was not started until 1846 and took several years to complete. Today, the site of the original Wills Eye Hospital is a parking lot across from the Academy of Natural Sciences on one side and the Cathedral of Saints Peter and Paul on the other.

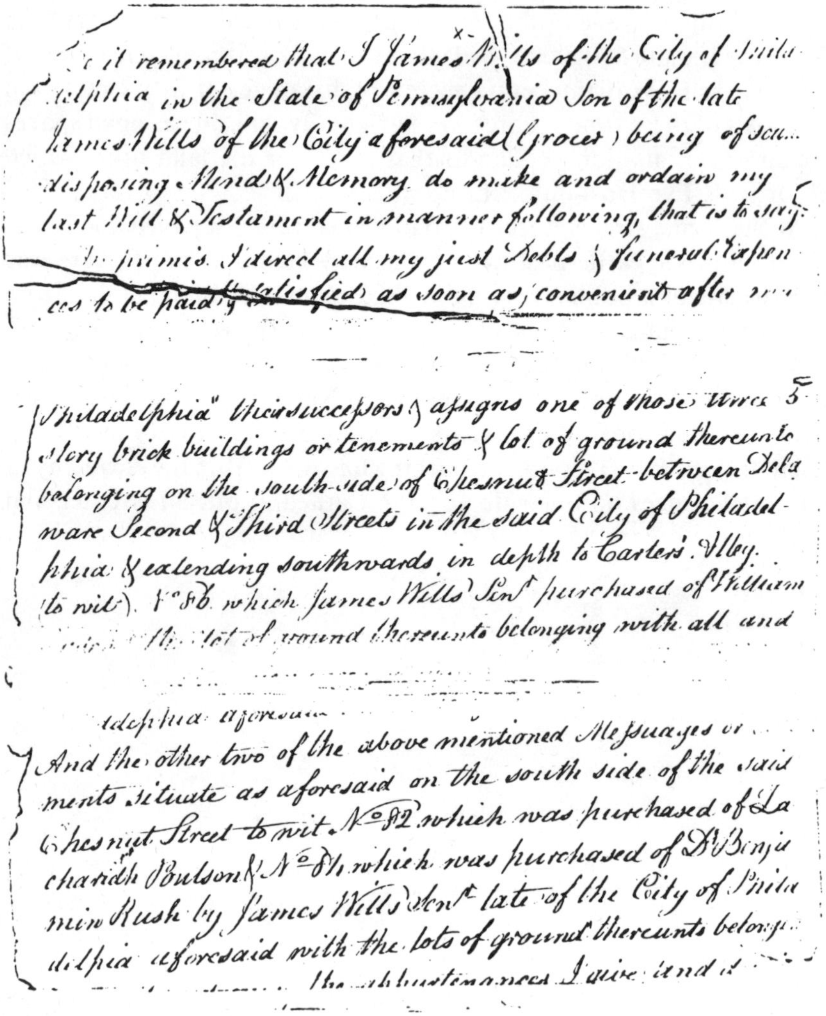

Be it remembered that I James Wills of the City of Phila-
delphia in the State of Pennsylvania Son of the late
James Wills of the City aforesaid (Grocer) being of sou...
disposing Mind & Memory do make and ordain my
last Will & Testament in manner following, that is to say:
In primis I direct all my just Debts & funeral expen
ces to be paid & satisfied as soon as convenient after m...

Philadelphia their successors & assigns one of those three
story brick buildings or tenements & lot of ground thereunto
belonging on the south side of Chesnut Street between Dela
ware Second & Third Streets in the said City of Philadel-
phia & extending southwards in depth to Carter's Alley.
(to wit) No 86 which James Wills Sin.r purchased of William
... the lot of ground thereunto belonging with all and

...delphia aforesaid.
And the other two of the above mentioned Messuages or ...
ments situate as aforesaid on the south side of the said
Chesnut Street to wit No 82 which was purchased of La
charitch Poulson & No 84 which was purchased of Dr Benja
min Rush by James Wills Sen.r late of the City of Phila
delphia aforesaid with the lots of ground thereunto belong...
the appurtenances I give and ...

Fig 1-7. Where it all began: the last will and testament of James Wills, Jr.

10

...nd accommodations for an ...ospital of ... ...

denominated "The Wills Hospital for the Relief of the Indigent Blind & Lame". The Funds thus appropriated are to be put out on good Mortgage security or City Stock, and after expending the necessary Sum for the Lot and improvements heretofore mentioned the income of the re-...

Fig 1-7 (*continued*).

11

Chapter 2

The First Hospital Building

The next question was to determine the builder and the design of the hospital. This decision was placed in the hands of a committee composed of men from City Council (named on November 1, 1831), all of whom were eminent Philadelphians: Messrs. Daniel Groves, Joshua Lippincott, and John Moss. Their first meeting was on April 20, 1832. Incidentally, the minutes shown in Fig 2-1 point out that a James Walker offered to serve as superintendent of the new hospital for the sum of $30 a month, considerably less than the 1980 rate. Another candidate, Samuel Steal, also volunteered to serve at this low rate. It must have been considered quite an honor to work for this newly founded institution.

To select a design for the new hospital, the committee sponsored a competition, to be judged by William J. Duane, Joshua Lippincott, John R. Neff, and the president of the Bricklayers Company, Daniel Groves, who had recently been elected to the council on October 11th. Risley, a famous Wills Eye surgeon, names others appointed to the committee (probably from Common Council): Joseph Worrell, R. McMullin, R. M. Huston, B. H. Yarnall, and Enoch Robbins, another member of the Bricklayers Company.

Several rising young architects competed in the contest. John Haviland, John C. Trautwine, William Rodrigue, George Seneff, and Thomas Ustick Walter all submitted designs for the hospital. The committee met on December 29 to reach a decision. After careful review, to Walter went the first prize of $100; to Trautwine, second prize of $50; and to Rodrigue, Seneff, and Haviland, $25 each

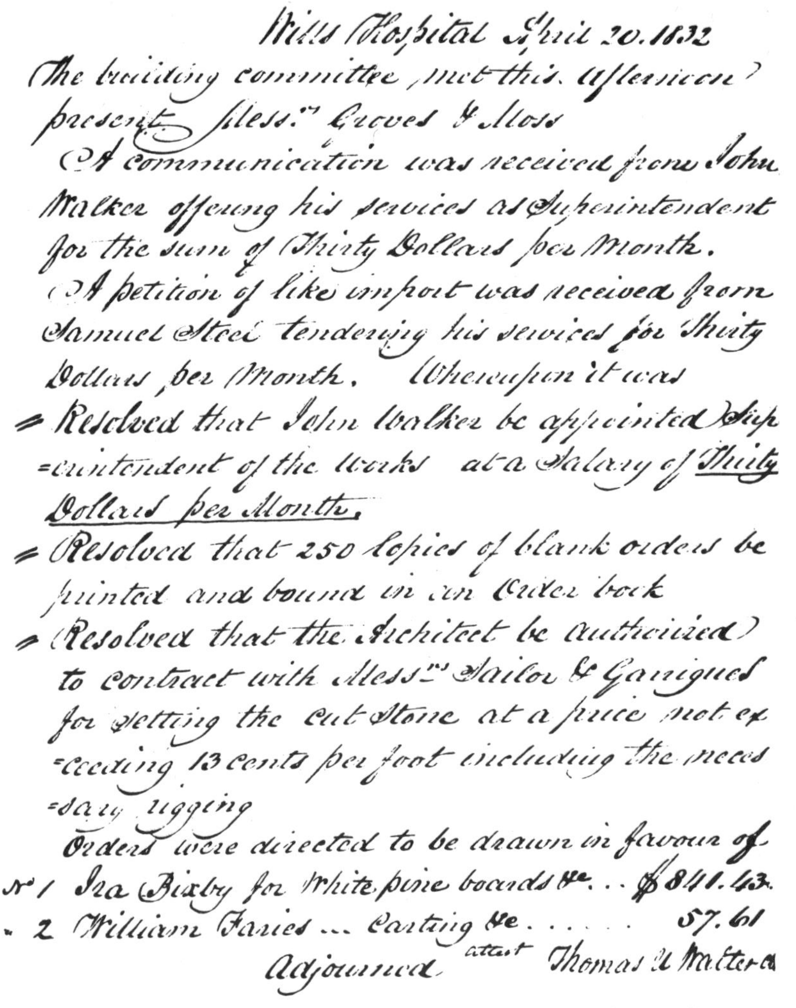

Wills Hospital April 20. 1832

The building committee, met this afternoon present Mess.' Groves & Moss

A communication was received from John Walker offering his services as Superintendent for the sum of Thirty Dollars per Month.

A petition of like import was received from Samuel Steel tendering his services for Thirty Dollars per Month. Whereupon it was

Resolved that John Walker be appointed Superintendent of the Works at a Salary of Thirty Dollars per Month.

Resolved that 250 copies of blank orders be printed and bound in an Order book

Resolved that the Architect be authorised to contract with Mess.' Sailor & Garrigues for setting the cut Stone at a price not exceeding 13 cents per foot including the necessary rigging

Orders were directed to be drawn in favour of
N.° 1 Ira Bixby for White pine boards &c. . . $841.43.
. 2 William Faries . . . Carting &c. 57.61
Adjourned attest Thomas U. Walter

Fig 2-1. The first committee meeting minutes of the Wills Hospital, April 20, 1832, written in longhand and signed by Thomas U. Walter.

(although, as Baigell points out, Haviland recorded receiving no less than $100, which may have been payment for his first, presumably solicited design presented in June). The results were published in the *Philadelphia Gazette and Daily Advertiser* on January 6 and were reprinted in *Poulson's American Daily Advertiser* the next day.

The original drawings Walter submitted on December 1, 1831, have been lost. However, among his papers are some fragments of a draft of his letter (dated November 26) accompanying the design which, when pieced together, reads as follows:

Gentlemen:

I herewith submit for your consideration a design for an "Asylum for the Lame and Blind," see [drawing] no. 1. By reference to the plan of Principal story you will observe that I have placed all the living rooms or dormitories in wings contiguous to the Centre building, in which I have made arrangement for Dining Room, Meeting Room etc. My object in making this disposition is, in the first place, to obtain the greatest accommodation at the least expenditure, [and] secondly, to have a dining room on the principal floor which in my opinion is a desideratum of considerable importance. The dining room in the Widows Asylum [by Strickland, 1819–1820] is in the Basement Story and from information received from the matron this arrangement completely destroys the comfort of the house.

Another object of importance gained by the disposition I have made, is the approach to all the dormitories, stairways, dining rooms, etc. from a straight passage or Corridor, which makes the establishment peculiarly adapted to the accommodation of the Blind. You will observe also that this manner of building ensures a free circulation of Air thro' all the rooms (see no. 2). I have made the dormitories 10 x 15 ft., supposing this to be sufficiently large for 2 persons. There are 40 dormitories. Consequently the building will contain 80 persons with the necessary accommodations for Steward, Matron, Physicians, Attendants, Kitchen, Washing Room, Ironing Room, Bath room, a room for Religious meeting, etc. In designing an edifice of this kind, it is necessary to have reference to a future enlargement of the establishment. With the design I offer for your consideration this may be advantageously effected. The Wings may be extended to any required distance and flanked by two end building symmetrical with the center, and, should the accommodations thus obtained prove insufficient at any future period, other ranges of dormitories may be constructed extending from each corner building at right angles with the front.

Walter's career had started out rather inauspiciously. Initially he was a bricklayer. However, taking advantage of architecture courses offered at the Franklin Institute, he ultimately became one of Philadelphia's leading architects. The high point in his professional life came in 1842, when he was appointed to the faculty of the Franklin Institute as professor of architecture. He also laid out the plans for Girard College and assisted Charles Pierre L'Enfant in designing the wings of the Senate and House of the United States Capitol in Washington, D.C.

Walter's design of Wills Eye Hospital was one of his first efforts. The committee considered him a novice, a fact that became evident in its report giving the reasons for its choice. They stated that judgment had been made from

consideration of all the circumstances connected with the legacy and the object, and not strictly from a regard of mere architectural merit. The fund is too limited to warrant such structures as some of the plans represent, so that economy as well as adequacy have been regarded in preference to display or beauty.

Final plans for the hospital were submitted to the city council and were approved by them on January 13, 1833 (Fig 2-2). The minutes of the Select Committee of Philadelphia state that plans and estimates for the new hospital were received on June 6, 1831. According to Hazard's Register (IX, 1), they were submitted by Haviland and Strickland. The committee, however, did not find them satisfactory, and they had to be redone.

There is some question as to when the cornerstone of the hospital was actually laid. The earlier *History of Wills Eye Hospital* states that it was April 2, 1832, but there is some doubt about whether this date is accurate, since the hospital building committee appointed by Philadelphia City Council did not meet until April 20, 1832 (Fig 2-1). We are sure, however, that the hospital was completed by 1834.

The completed building was 80 feet long and 50 feet deep. On the south side there was a piazza approximately 12 feet wide. The hospital was built to accommodate approximately 70 patients and consisted of

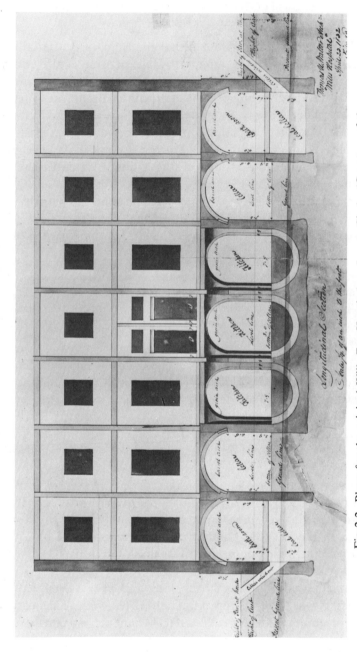

Fig 2-2. Plans for the original Wills Eye Hospital on Logan Circle. (Courtesy of the Athenaeum of Philadelphia, private collection.)

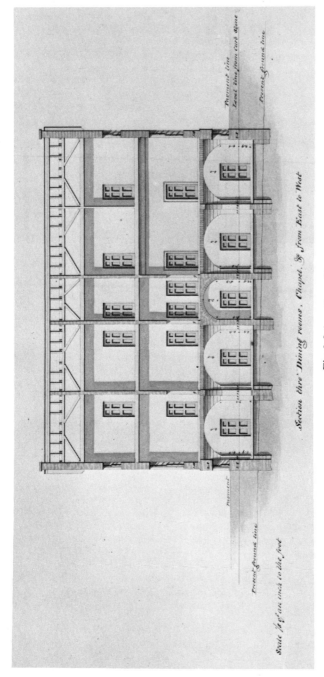

Section thro.' Dining rooms, Chapel. &.c from East to West

Fig 2-2 (*continued*).

17

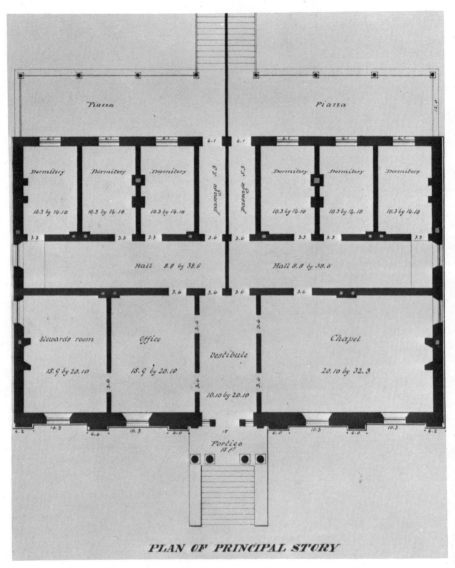

Fig 2-2 (*continued*).

three stories: basement, first floor, and second floor, with an attic 24 feet wide and 80 feet long. The roof was made of copper, and the lot was surrounded by a cut stone fence 2 feet high, upon which was placed an iron railing. The front of the building on Race Street was made of sandstone and featured six ionic pilasters (Fig 2-3). Surrounding the front door was a Grecian ionic portico consisting of four columns (Fig 2-4).

The hospital opened on March 3, 1834, and Joseph R. Ingersoll gave the dedication address. In the midst of all the preparations, however, the hospital founders began to question the intentions of James Wills. Was the institution to be a hospital for the treatment of the blind or lame or should it become an asylum for the incapacitated? Fortunately, the committee voted in favor of continuing as a hospital, because it was their feeling that an asylum could care for only 12 to 15 people, while a hospital could treat thousands.

On April 1, 1834, the hospital committee reported that the Wills Eye Hospital had opened in March 1834 (Fig 2-5). The report shows that 10

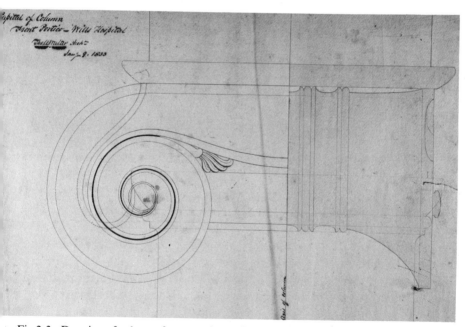

Fig 2-3. Drawing of column, front portico, Wills Hospital. (Drawing in possession of Girard College.)

19

Fig 2-4. Two little children wait outside the original Wills Eye Hospital, created as an asylum for the blind, lame, and indigent. This hospital, located on Logan Square, reflects the architectural style of the 19th century.

patients were submitted for medical or surgical care, while 10 others were apparently turned away because it was felt that they could not be helped.

Isaac Parrish (Joseph's son) performed the first cataract operation at Wills Eye Hospital, a fact recorded in the report of April 1, 1834 (Fig 2-5). At the time of the report, the outcome of the surgery was not known, but Rodman Paul and Charles Stout were optimistic that the operation would be successful.

As expected, the expenditures of the day were somewhat less than what we encounter in our inflationary society of 1980. Only $247.36 was spent in the month covered by the report; this included bread and milk, as well as medicines, which were felt would last "several months." The committee than recommended that $20, in addition to the $5.37 already in the hands of the steward, be appropriated for current expenses during the month of April. Of interest, too, is a notation in

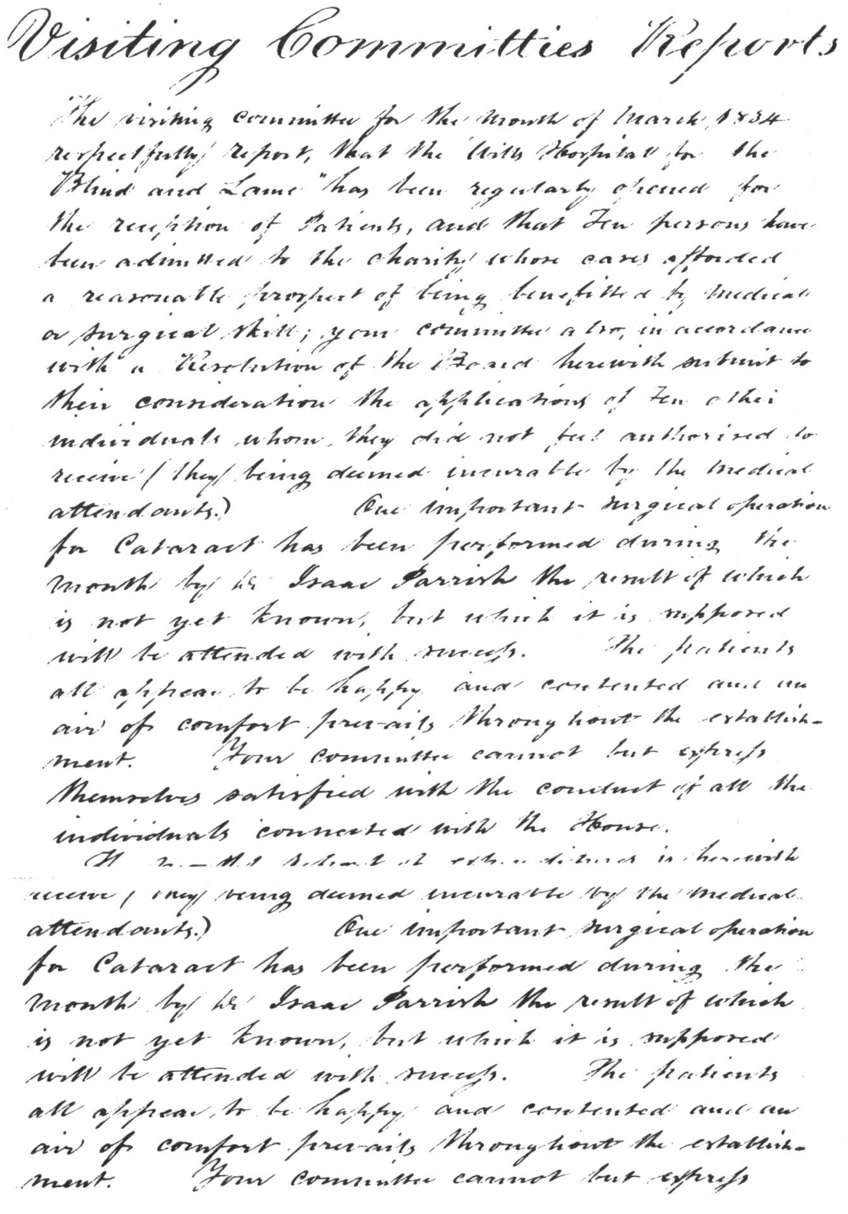

Visiting Committies Reports

The visiting committee for the month of March, 1834 respectfully report, that the "Wills Hospital for the Blind and Lame" has been regularly opened for the reception of Patients, and that Ten persons have been admitted to the charity whose cases afforded a reasonable prospect of being benefitted by medical or surgical skill; your committee also, in accordance with a Resolution of the Board herewith submit to their consideration the applications of Ten other individuals whom they did not feel authorized to receive (they being deemed incurable by the medical attendants.) One important surgical operation for Cataract has been performed during the month by Dr. Isaac Parrish the result of which is not yet known, but which it is supposed will be attended with success. The patients all appear to be happy and contented and an air of comfort prevails throughout the establishment. Your committee cannot but express themselves satisfied with the conduct of all the individuals connected with the House.

It is — that submit of other individuals is herewith receive (they being deemed incurable by the medical attendants.) One important surgical operation for Cataract has been performed during the month by Dr. Isaac Parrish the result of which is not yet known, but which it is supposed will be attended with success. The patients all appear to be happy and contented and an air of comfort prevails throughout the establishment. Your committee cannot but express

Fig 2-5. Excerpts from the minutes of the visiting committee report, March 1834. The minutes refer to the first cataract operation at the Wills.

the final paragraph that alterations be made in the south portico of the building to prevent deterioration of the plaster from rain. As with all new buildings, past and present, defects creep up even shortly after completion.

The City Council of Philadelphia managed the hospital until 1869, when the Board of Directors of City Trusts took over. While still under the aegis of City Council, a board of managers, composed of 18 members, none of whom were members of the council, were charged with the responsibility of managing Wills Eye Hospital, 31 of whom were physicians. In addition, there were five presidents of the board of managers during the period before 1869; three of them were physicians. The first, of course, was Dr. Joseph Parrish, who served from December 2, 1833, to March 2, 1840. He was succeeded by Dr. Frederick Eringer, who resigned in 1843, to be followed by Dr. J. Rodman Paul, who served from 1843 to 1864, when he resigned. Next in line was Dr. Andrew Nevinger, who served for only a little over a year and was not reappointed. The final president of this period was Charles Ellis (not a physician), who assumed that position in December 1865 and then went on to become a member of the Board of Directors of City Trusts.

Chapter 3

The Early Surgeons

Isaac Parrish was born in Philadelphia in 1811. Son of the first president of the board of managers of Wills Eye Hospital, Joseph Parrish, he was one of 11 children and was educated in a Friends school. He later matriculated at the University of Pennsylvania and was graduated with a medical degree in 1832. After further training at the Philadelphia Hospital, he became one of the first surgeons at the Wills Eye Hospital at the young age of 23. He is credited with performing its first cataract operation. He also lectured extensively on ophthalmology and was generally well liked by his colleagues.

Parrish was very active in the Society for the Abolition of Slavery and was also interested in improving the plight of prisoners. He was still a young man when he died in 1852 of dysentery, which he contracted from his eldest son, who had been ill for several weeks. Both father and son died in the same hour. This tragedy deprived society of a dedicated individual who undoubtedly would have made even greater contributions to mankind had he lived longer.

As an aside, the Parrish family includes a well-known artist of the day. Maxfield Parrish was Isaac Parrish's greatnephew, son of Stephen Parrish, who was the son of Dillwyn Parrish, Isaac Parrish's brother. Maxfield Parrish's chemistry notebook from Haverford College testifies to his playfulness and good spirit (Fig 3-1). The same spirit is evident in his mural of "Old King Cole," originally the bar mural of John Jacob Astor's Knickerbocker Hotel in New York City and now displayed in the St. Regis' barroom. The joke behind the King Cole mural is that the good king had just committed an unkingly faux

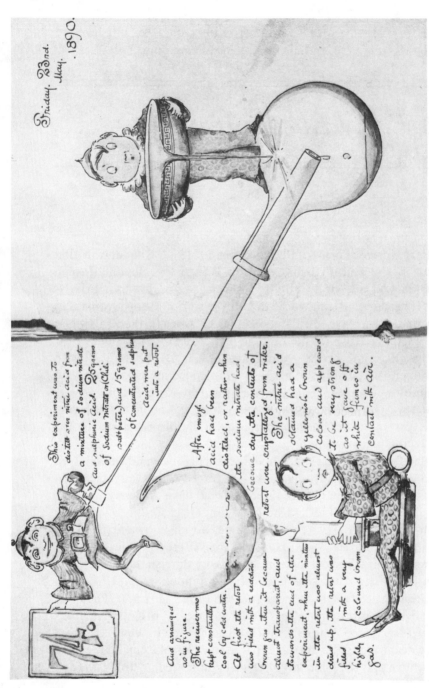

Fig 3-1. There are different ways to approach chemistry, as Maxfield Parrish, greatnephew of Isaac Parrish, shows. Elves clutch the bunsen burner and slide down the breakers he used in his chemistry experiments. Unfortunately, his artwork did not earn him any points in chemistry. His grade for the course was only 68!

pas—flatus ejectus. How do we know? King Cole is leaning more to one side than the other and his face seems to be saying "I didn't really do that." Also, his court is in an upheaval. Jesters are frolicking, a page boy is blushing, and the fiddlers look amazed. And Parrish's only comment when asked about the painting was "When I painted it my thoughts were 110 per cent pure!"

The Parrish family has indeed made rather interesting contributions to the city of Philadelphia.

Squier Littel

Squier Littel was another of the four surgeons appointed to Wills Eye Hospital. Squier Littel was born in Burlington, New Jersey, in 1803. His ancestors had come from London, England, and had settled initially in Newberry, Massachusetts, in 1630. From that point, the family scattered throughout the East and Middle West.

Both of Squier's parents died while he was a young child, so he was adopted by an uncle, Dr. Squier Littel, of Butler, Ohio. Inspired by his uncle to enter medicine, he came to Philadelphia in 1821, where he studied under the guidance of Dr. Joseph Parrish. He entered medical school at the University of Pennsylvania and was graduated in 1824. His graduation thesis was entitled "Inflammation."

Squier Littel was an adventurous soul and was soon lured to Buenos Aires by the prospect of a South American adventure. Disillusioned and homesick, he stayed for only about 4 months before returning to Philadelphia by way of Chile, Peru, and Ecuador. On his return to Philadelphia, Littel became an active member of a committee to revise and correct an edition of the *Book of Common Prayer*. He also was editor of "The Banner of the Cross," one of the most influential church papers of the times, and wrote poetry and metrical translations of medieval hymns.

Littel's contributions to medicine were many and varied. They included editorship of three volumes of the *Journal of Foreign Medicine* as well as contributions to the *American Journal of the Medical Sciences*. He also wrote a textbook entitled *A Manual of Diseases of the Eye*, which was published in 1837. This was a clearly written, concise work that was later revised in 1838 by Hugh Houston, a member of the Royal College of Surgeons in London.

In 1854, he edited an American edition of H. Hayes Waldman's

Operative Ophthalmic Surgery. This innovative text recommended chloroform over ether and suggested its use for patients of all ages as an agent that would "tranquilize the mind, deaden the sensibility . . . , while to the operator it assured complete command of the patient." As it turned out, however, general anesthesia was not the great boon to the ophthalmic surgeon that it was to the general surgeon. Too often, vomiting and retching impeded or complicated the recovery following ocular surgery. There was no way, certainly, for Littel to have known this, and there is no doubt that he was very concerned about making advancements in the field of ophthalmology.

It is reported that late in life he developed choroiditis and failing sight before he died of cardiorenal problems at the age of 83. His contributions to the Wills Eye Hospital also included his son-in-law and assistant, Dr. A. D. Hall, who served as an active member on the Wills Eye Hospital Staff.

Isaac Hays

The third representative to the staff of the Wills Eye Hospital was Isaac Hays. Hays was the only Jewish physician on the staff. He was born in 1796 and on his mother's side was a descendant of the well-known Gratz family. His aunt, Rebecca Gratz, was the model for Rebecca in *Ivanhoe.*

How Rebecca Gratz of Philadelphia became the model for Scott's Rebecca is a story worth telling. Rebecca Gratz had become a good friend of Tilly Hoffman, a daughter of a New York judge, and had visited her numerous times in New York City. Unfortunately, Tilly developed tuberculosis, of which she died at the age of 18. During her illness, she was visited many times by Rebecca, who thereby made the acquaintance of another visitor, Washington Irving. Irving was in love with Tilly and spent many hours at her bedside. He was charmed by Rebecca's beauty and grace. After Tilly's death, Irving met Walter Scott during a trip to Europe. Coincidentally, Scott told Irving that he was planning a book that included some Jewish characters. Irving, remembering the beauty and character of Rebecca Gratz, described her to Scott, who subsequently created the famous heroine of *Ivanhoe.* Had this book been written today rather than in the 19th century, it is very possible that Wilfred of Ivanhoe might have chosen to marry

Rebecca rather than Rowena. The prospect of interfaith marriage at that time, of course, was extremely unlikely.

Upon completion of his novel, Scott wrote to Irving and asked "What do you think of your Rebecca—did I follow the pattern?" The answer was yes.

Issac Hays' father had been a successful merchant who had hoped that his son would follow in his footsteps. However, Isaac was more interested in medicine, and he graduated from the University of Pennsylvania Medical School in 1820. Initially engaged in general practice, he began more and more to devote himself to the study and treatment of diseases of the eye. With Squier Littel, he became one of the pioneers in American ophthalmology. Like Littel, he was a good writer and ultimately became editor of the *American Journal of Medical Sciences.*

Isaac Hays married Sarah Minus, and their son, Isaac Minus Hays, also became a physician and later joined his father in practice; father and son were coeditors of the *American Journal of the Medical Sciences* for 75 years. As editor, Hays had the right to refuse any manuscript. However, he was a courteous gentleman, and it became well known that a casual greeting to someone who had submitted a manuscript usually meant that the paper had been accepted, while obsequious behavior meant that the paper had been turned down. By such conduct Hays hoped to lighten the blow of rejection.

Some landmark papers that appeared in the *Journal* included Horner's original description in 1824 of the small muscles at the internal commissure of the eyelids, as well as an ingenious operation described by Horner for correction of ectropion of the lower lid.

Hays became a close friend of Joseph Parrish and continued as a surgeon at the Wills Eye Hospital until 1854, when pressures of his editorship forced him to resign. However, he continued to contribute quarterly reports of the work done on his service at the Wills Eye Hospital; these were published in the *American Journal of the Medical Sciences.*

Isaac Hays was also very interested in natural history and contributed many articles in this field. One of them was a masterful work on the mastodon. As a result of this interest, he was made president of the Academy of Natural Sciences in Philadelphia in 1865. He also became an honorary member of the American Ophthalmological

Society at its first meeting in 1864 and received honors from the Medical Society at Hamburg, the Société Universelle d'Ophthalmologie, and the Congrés Medicale Internationale de Paris. A respected member of the community, he died in 1879 at the age of 83.

George Fox

The final member of the original foursome was George Fox, the youngest son of 13 children born to Samuel Mickel Fox. He was born in 1806 and was a member of the Society of Friends. He was a graduate of Philadelphia private schools and, like his colleagues, attended the University of Pennsylvania, receiving his medical degree in 1820. He was another of Dr. Joseph Parrish's distinguished pupils. While a resident physician at the Pennsylvania Hospital, he devised an apparatus for the treatment of fractures of the clavicle. He was not a prolific writer, but he did bring the work of Wills Eye Hospital to the attention of the medical profession by publishing clinical reports in the *American Journal of Medical Sciences* in November 1839.

Though interested in diseases of the eye, he was against subspecialization and did not wish to be known only as an ophthalmologist. In 1854, he retired and left the city to live in the country. He was a good businessman and had been able to acquire a sizable fortune at a young age, as well as a directorship of the National Bank of Commerce in 1876, a position he held until his death. A philanthropist, he was also active in obtaining a building at Thirteenth and Locust Streets for the College of Physicians. He died in 1882 at the age of 76.

Chapter 4

Wills Eye Hospital in the 19th Century

The 19th century was a good era for Wills Eye Hospital. Physicians famous in their own right and those who fathered famous sons passed through the portals of this growing medical center. Some were known as surgeons, others as pioneers in the technology of ophthalmology; still others had sons who achieved fame in the military or the arts. Their stories are unusual and deserve special attention.

George B. McClellan

George B. McClellan (Fig 4-1) was born in Woodstock, Connecticut, on December 23, 1796. McClellan was a famous surgeon as well as the father of General George B. MClellan of Civil War fame. A graduate of Yale University at the age of 15, he later attended the University of Pennsylvania Medical School. He was an enthusiastic student, particularly interested in anatomy. Shortly after graduation from medical school, he and some associates started a private school of anatomy, later known as Jefferson Medical College. One reason McClellan started a new medical school was that there were no available positions at the University of Pennsylvania, where he doubtless would have liked to teach. McClellan therefore served as a professor of surgery at the new Jefferson Medical College, and his skill as a surgeon and teacher were unsurpassed.

In 1821, McClellan, though a general surgeon, founded still another institution, a hospital for diseases of the eye and ear. Unfortunately, however, this survived for only 4 years. To add to his bad luck, in 1838

Fig 4-1. George B. McClellan.

the Jefferson Medical College reorganized and McClellan was not reappointed to the staff.

McClellan was dynamic and active and liked to be in the forefront of his profession. However, he had a bombastic personality and probably talked too much. It is said that at the time of his death he had virtually no friends.

McClellan was involved in what almost certainly was the first malpractice suit that involved a staff member of the Wills Eye Hospital; in fact, it may have been one of the first malpractice suits in the United States. The suit arose when a Dr. Beattie spread rumors that

McClellan had mistreated one William Davis. The suit came to trial and in his testimony, Davis said:

> On December 26, 1821, I went to the hospital [Wills Eye Hospital], where Dr. Parrish operated on my left eye. I lost the eye. On May 22, 1822, Dr. Parrish operated on my right eye. An inflammation followed and I remained in the Hospital until 1823.

Obviously no utilization review committee existed in those days!

It appears that both operations on Mr. Davis were cataract procedures, one eye having been approached with a couching technique and the other probably by extraction. Davis went on to explain that he had taken a blind man to McClellan's office. After examining the blind man, McClellan examined Davis. After looking at his most recently operated eye, he advised surgery. Although Mr. Davis later testified that he had been advised by Dr. Parrish not to let anyone operate on his eye, the eye later became sore and Dr. McClellan ultimately operated in Davis' boardinghouse bedroom. Davis stated that that was the last time he had any sight in his second eye.

At the trial the relative merits of both the couching and the extraction operation were discussed. Dr. Parrish testified that he had performed only one such extraction and that the patient had lost his eye. He went on to point out that Baron Wenzel, a famous German surgeon, had lost a hatful of eyes before he became proficient in the extraction technique. The court discussed the different methods, and it was noted that Dr. Parrish performed only the more common types of operations: needling and couching. Dr. Burton Chance writes that the suit was finally settled between McClellan and Davis for $500, a considerable amount of money in those days.

McClellan's son, General Brinton McClellan, actually became more famous than his father, although many felt that if the surgeon had been the general, the army would have won more battles and fought more often, thereby shortening the duration of the Civil War. George Brinton McClellan was born in Philadelphia in 1826 and was graduated from the United States Military Academy in 1846, second in his class. He served in the Mexican War and in 1855 went to Europe as a member of the commission to study the European military systems. While there, he had the opportunity to observe part of the Crimean War. In 1857, McClellan resigned from the army and became chief engineer of the Illinois Central Railroad. He was to become its vice president before moving on to become president of the eastern division of the Ohio and Mississippi Railroad.

At the outbreak of the Civil War, McClellan enlisted and became a major general in command of Ohio volunteers. After defeating all the Confederate forces in western Virginia, he was made a major general in the regular United States Army. In the summer of 1861, he took command of the Union Army in the East, which became known as the Army of the Potomac. Under his exemplary leadership, it became one of the best forces in the Union Army. At the height of his career, McClellan was chief of all the armies in the Union. However, despite his proven military skill, President Lincoln thought that he was not aggressive enough against the Confederates and relieved him as supreme general early in 1862.

McClellan did remain in the service as an army commander. In the spring of 1862, he attacked, moving against Richmond from the east in the Peninsular Campaign. Lee retaliated in the Battle of Seven Days and drove him back to Harris' Landing on the James River. Washington authorities transferred McClellan's army to northern Virginia. Most of his troops were placed temporarily under the command of General John Pope, who, in turn, was defeated at the second battle of Bull Run, also called Manassis. McClellan then became commander of all troops in the Washington area. He led his army into Maryland to meet a Confederate invasion and forced the southern army to retreat to Virginia in the Battle of Antietem (September 1862), the bloodiest 1-day battle of the Civil War. Lincoln, however, was displeased with McClellan's failure to follow up on his victory and to deal Lee and the Confederates a death blow. McClellan was replaced by General Ambrose Burnside, and his military career ended. Nonetheless, Lee respected McClellan as one of the Union's most talented field commanders.

Despite his military career misadventures, McClellan was well liked by his troops, who affectionately called him "Little Mac." A man of short stature, his height of 5'7" or 5'8" contrasted dramatically with that of President Lincoln, especially when the latter wore his stovepipe hat (Fig 4-2).

In 1864, McClellan ran unsuccessfully against Lincoln for the presidency. He later became governor of New Jersey, serving from 1868 to 1872. His son, also George McClellan, followed in his father's footsteps; associated with Tammany Hall, he also served as a U.S. senator from New York and as mayor of New York.

Fig 4-2. Abe Lincoln and "Little Mac" George McClellan stand face to face.

Fitzwilliam Sargent

Fitzwilliam Sargent is better known as the father of a famous artist, John Singer Sargent, than for his accomplishments as an ophthalmologist. Born on May 17, 1829, he was part of an English family of military, political, and artistic accomplishments. Fitzwilliam Sargent, in the tradition of his successful family, graduated from the University of Pennsylvania Medical School in 1843, by which time he was already on the staff of the Wills Eye Hospital. He is best known for a book entitled *Bandaging and Other Operations of Minor Surgery*, which was published in several editions and was also translated into French and Japanese. He also edited a few books on surgery and, in 1862, while living in France, wrote a pamphlet entitled "England, The United States, and the Southern Confederacy" in defense of the Union cause.

Sargent married Mary Newbold Singer in 1850. She was the talented daughter of a local merchant and had spent much of her early life in Italy. She was artistic and an accomplished musician. At her insistence, Sargent, who had been an attending surgeon at the Wills Eye Hospital since 1852, resigned in 1854 at the young age of 34, allegedly because of poor health. It is reported that he had earned enough money from his practice to retire at this early age. In any case, his health had to have been better than he supposed because Sargent lived another 35 years. He did not die until he had reached the ripe old age of 69.

Shortly after his retirement, the family moved to Florence, Italy, where his son, John Singer Sargent, was born in 1856. Fitzwilliam Sargent hoped that his son would enter the U.S. Navy, but Mrs. Sargent and friends persuaded him to nurture the boy's obvious artistic talents. At the age of 13, John went to work in the studio of Carl Welsch in Rome.

His natural gifts were immense. The violinist Joachim observed that "had Sargent taken to music instead of painting he would have been as great a musician as he was a painter." He called him "the van Dyke of our times." His teacher, Carolus-Duran, the foremost portraitist in Paris, offered him the considerable compliment of an invitation to join him in decorating a ceiling in the Louvre. Each incorporated a portrait of the other in the painting. Carolus-Duran lived to regret asking Sargent to participate because he soon found that critical acclaim at the annual Paris Salon (on which depended lucrative portrait commissions for the following year) was lavished more upon the pupil than the teacher.

One of the earliest and most important of Sargent's Salon pieces was exhibited in 1883, under the title "Portrait d'Enfants." This was actually the portrait of the four daughters of the American expatriate artist Edward Boit, painted the year before in the family apartment in Paris. It was the first large painting in which Sargent's personal and peculiar traits manifested themselves.

Basing the composition on "Las Meninas" of Velazquez, which he had copied in Spain (the copy still belongs to his sister's family), it is his first masterwork that shows his passion for objects and materials—the Savonnerie carpet in the foreground and the vast Chinese blue and white vases that add a mysterious timelessness to the work. It was subsequently presented by his sisters to the Boston Museum of Fine Arts.

In 1884, Sargent, continuing in his steady rise to fame, showed a major portrait in the Royal Academy of London summer exhibition. This exhibition brought the same sort of portrait patronage in England as it did in France. Again, his sitter was American, and again the painting had been finished in Paris. But, fortunately for Sargent, his subject, Mrs. Henry White, had moved to London, where her husband was secretary to the U.S. embassy. She had furnished a fashionable mansion in Grovesner Crescent, where, after the Royal Academy Show, the Sargent portrait was placed in the White Dining Room, a companion to the portrait of Henry White, which had been completed by the more famous and much older Leon Bonnet.

Sargent established a studio in London's Chelsea district in 1885 and was for 40 years the accepted master in Anglo-American portraiture.

In 1888, John Singer Sargent painted Isabella Stewart Gardner, who by her will established the Isabella Stewart Gardner Museum in Boston, Massachusetts. She was extremely friendly with Sargent, as evidenced by a collection of nearly 200 letters from him in her museum. Most are concerned with Mrs. Gardner's various acts of kindness.

Sargent's portrait of Mrs. Gardner shows her in a low-necked black dress against a piece of red and gold brocade (Fig 4-3). The pattern around her head is fitted with exact symmetry. From each of the three rows of pearls around her waist hangs one of her rubies.

Records indicate that this painting turned out to be something of an

Fig 4-3. Sargent's famous portrait of Isabella Stewart Gardner that (in 1888) was considered so "risque" by her husband.

ordeal for Sargent. Apparently he completed nine paintings before the last was finally acceptable to her. Some sources also say that the portrait created considerable scandal in the Boston area and that her husband forbade its showing in his lifetime.

D. Hayes Agnew

D. Hayes Agnew, the only child of Robert Agnew and Agnes Anderson, was one of the first surgeons to bring fame to Wills Eye Hospital because of his skill as an ophthalmic surgeon. Agnew, like most of Wills' early surgeons, was a graduate of the University of Pennsylvania. He married Margaret Creighton Irwin on November 21, 1841, and in 1843 gave up the practice of medicine to join his brother-in-law in the iron business. The business failed and he returned to medicine, this time in Cochranville.

He was determined to become a surgeon and had cadavers transported from Philadelphia to Cochranville, where, much to the dismay of local villagers, he performed his dissections. One legend about Agnew and his cadavers is that a farmer approached him and asked if he could put the bones from Agnew's cadavers into his fish pond. Subsequently, one of the local fish dealers became well known for the unusually fat eels that he regularly had for sale. The same farmer who had used Agnew's bones in his fish pond asked how the fish dealer managed to procure so many eels. To his dismay, he learned that they came from his very own pond. This and other tales about Agnew ultimately forced him to leave Cochranville.

In 1848, he returned to Philadelphia, where he purchased a school of anatomy for $600. At the time of purchase there was an enrollment of only nine students, but because of his energies and teaching abilities, students from the University of Pennsylvania and Jefferson Medical School were quick to enroll. When he later sold the school at no profit, the student body had increased to 50 students. In 1862, Agnew became acting surgeon to Satterly Hospital and traveled to Gettysburg, where he treated the wounded after that historic battle.

To increase his skill in eye surgery, Agnew applied for a position at Wills Eye Hospital and was appointed the 13th attending surgeon. He served for 4 years and then was emeritus surgeon until his death. He became a dominant force in medicine in Philadelphia and, indeed, in surgery throughout the United States. He influenced ophthalmology by the Agnew peritomy operation and the Agnew linear cataract extraction. He also developed a flexible canaliculus knife and a double hook for removing the lens nucleus when it could not be expressed spontaneously. Agnew was a severe critic of the couching operation and advised against using the linear operation in senile cataracts because of poor early results. His most significant contribution was a three-volume treatise on surgery, including a section on ophthalmology over 140 pages long.

At the height of Agnew's popularity, James Garfield became president of the United States. Garfield, a Republican, was in many ways a compromise candidate for president. The Republican party at that time was divided into two factions: the "Stalwarts," led by Senator Roscoe Conkling of New York, and the "Half-Breeds," led by Senator James G. Blaine of Maine. These groups quarreled over personal differences and government jobs rather than over political principles. Though Garfield was closer to the Half-Breeds, he tried to walk a fine line between both factions and therefore kept some of the confidence of both sides.

At the Republican National Convention in Chicago, the Half-Breeds tried to nominate Blaine for president, while the Stalwarts backed former President Ulysses S. Grant. Neither Blaine nor Grant could muster enough votes for the nomination, so the Half-Breeds turned to Garfield as a dark horse candidate. After 36 ballots, the convention finally chose Garfield. Chester A. Arthur, member of the Stalwart group and Conkling's lieutenant in the Republican regime, was selected as his vice-presidential running mate. In 1880, Garfield defeated his Democratic opponent, Winfield Scott Hancock, by about 40,000 votes (4,453,285 to 4,414,082).

After assuming office, Garfield, who owed his nomination primarily to the Half-Breeds, favored this faction in handing out patronage jobs. He made their leader, Blaine, his secretary of state and appointed several others to important offices. The Stalwarts received only minor positions and their leader, Conkling, tried to stop the Senate from confirming some of the appointments. He failed, however, and was forced to resign from the Senate.

On July 2, 1881, Garfield was about to leave Washington to attend the 25th reunion of his class at Williams College (prior to becoming president, he had been president of his alma mater). As he stood at the railroad station, a stranger stepped out of the crowd and fired two pistol shots at him. Garfield fell, and the assassin cried "I am a Stalwart and Arthur is president now!"

The assassin, Charles J. Guiteau, was arrested immediately. He held a grudge because Garfield had refused to appoint him as the US consul in Paris. At his trial, Guiteau tried to act like a madman and his attorney argued that he was innocent by reason of insanity. However, a jury found him guilty and he was hanged in 1882.

Garfield lingered for 80 days. While one of the assassin's bullets had merely grazed his arm, the other had lodged in his back. Roentgen had not yet discovered x-rays, and surgeons could not find the bullet. Even Alexander Graham Bell tried, unsuccessfully, to locate it with an electrical device.

Agnew, as one of the outstanding surgeons in the United States, was called into consultation on July 3, two days after Garfield had been shot. He left immediately for Washington in a private train, which made a record run of less than 3 hours. Agnew was ceaseless in his attention to President Garfield, and it was the opinion of the authorities that Garfield had received the best possible treatment. Undoubtedly, had radiology, antibiotics, and modern surgical techniques existed, Garfield's life would have been saved. Unfortunately, infection set in, and Garfield died at a seaside cottage in Elberon, New Jersey, on September 19, 1881.

Thus, D. Hayes Agnew added to the prestige of Wills Eye Hospital not only through his contributions to ophthalmology but also as a consultant to President James Garfield.

Other Key Surgeons

There were many other respected surgeons who practiced ophthalmology in the 1800s. Richard Levis, a graduate of the Jefferson Medical College, was a general surgeon who was known for his personal neatness and habit of entering the operating room without changing clothes. He was probably one of the best-dressed surgeons of the day and took great pride in showing off his cuffs during surgery. He was particularly proud of the fact that even in the bloodiest of operations, he always managed to keep his cuffs spotless. Upon completion of the operation, he would wash his hands, adjust his bow tie, and make rounds on his private patients.

His operative dexterity added to the prestige of the institution. In addition, he is credited with the development of the wire lens loupe for delivery of the lens during cataract surgery.

These early surgeons had the difficult task of performing ophthalmic operations with the crudest of techniques and equipment. Wills Eye has, however, always been known for its excellent cataract extractions, as well as for its superb plastic work. Recessions and resections of the rectus muscles for strabismus were unknown. As an alternative, complete tenotomies of the horizontal recti were frequently performed, which, needless to say, frequently made eyes that turned out turn in, and eyes that turned in turn out. Fortunately, the vertical recti were apparently spared this fate.

The surgical treatment of glaucoma did not begin until 1856, when von Graefe devised the technique of iridectomy. Before this time there were no anesthetics, either local or general. Thus the surgeon was extremely limited in what he could accomplish.

Two exciting discoveries changed the course of ophthalmic surgery. The first was the development of the ophthalmoscope by Helmholtz in 1851, and the second was the development of the indirect ophthalmoscope by Reute in 1852. Because of these developments, by 1860 ophthalmology had emerged as a recognized subspecialty.

Following the Civil War, it became the fashion for physicians to study in Europe and then return to the United States as ophthalmic specialists. Notable among surgeons who did this were Dyer, Kaiser, Norris, Strawbridge, and Thompson. William Norris and William Thompson, both Wills Eye surgeons, spent 5 years in Vienna and then came back to teach at the University of Pennsylvania.

Two other surgeons, Hall and Harlan, were elected surgeons at the Wills Eye Hospital, at a time earlier than that of Levis and Agnew. After the Civil War, both confined their work to diseases of the eye. These two, therefore, were probably the first specialists at the Wills Eye who can be considered strictly ophthalmologists. Dyer, Kaiser, McClure, Norris, Thompson, and Strawbridge followed quickly in their stead.

William Fisher Norris and William Thompson

William Fisher Norris lived between 1839 and 1901. His parents came from Quaker stock, and Norristown was named after his family.

A member of the Society of Friends, he joined the Union Army, and from July 1 to July 3, 1863, he worked constantly at taking care of the wounded at the Battle of Gettysburg. Later he served at the Douglass Hospital in Washington, and with William Thompson he helped found the Army Medical Museum. He spent 5 years studying in Vienna under the guidance of Jaeger and later came back to work at the Wills Eye Hospital with George Strawbridge. In 1874 he became the first professor of ophthalmology at the University of Pennsylvania, where the present chair of ophthalmology carries both his name and that of Dr. George deSchweinitz. He was a president of the American Ophthalmological Society. His comprehensive textbook of ophthalmology was translated into many foreign languages.

Dr. Norris was married to Fräulein Rose Buchmann, a woman he met while a student in Vienna. They had three sons, one of whom died early in life. One of the remaining sons became a teacher and the other a lawyer.

William Thompson, a contemporary of William Fisher Norris, came from Chambersburg, Pennsylvania. A graduate of Jefferson Medical College, he was a lover of music. Like Norris, he served in the Civil War on the staff of General McClellan during the Peninsular campaign and at Antietam. A successful specialist, he was associated with Drs. S. Weir Mitchell and W.W. Keen and participated in many of their projects. One of these was a paper on eye strain entitled "Eye and its Association with Headache," written with Mitchell and published in 1874. In the preceding year he had written about the diagnosis of brain tumors by use of the ophthalmoscope. An authority on the optics of refraction, he invented several new instruments, including a type of refractor. He was also an authority on color blindness.

Thompson was a contemporary of the famous Philadelphia painter Thomas Aikens. Aikens had always maintained a keen interest in anatomy; in addition to his studies at the Pennsylvania Academy of the Fine Arts, he studied anatomy at the Jefferson Medical College. At one point, he even considered becoming a physician. His famous 1874 painting of the Gross Clinic still hangs at the Jefferson Medical College, although at the time of its unveiling it was severely criticized because of the blood shown on the fingers of Dr. Gross.

Aikens also painted Dr. William Thompson, and that painting now hangs in the College of Physicians in Philadelphia. It was painted in 1907, the year Thompson died.

Of interest is the fact that Aikens received only about $15,000 for all of his paintings. Many portraits he simply gave away. Today, just one of his paintings commands considerably more than $15,000.

Samuel Doty Risley

Many other Wills surgeons became well known, and certainly one cannot fail to mention Samuel Doty Risley, born in Cincinnati in 1845. Risley grew up in Cincinnati and in Davenport, Iowa. At the age of 17, stirred by the patriotic impluses of the period, he enlisted with the 20th regiment of Iowa volunteers. He enlisted on August 12, 1862, and by January 23, 1863, had been promoted to eighth corporal. He rose to fourth sergeant by May 23, 1865, before being mustered out in Mobile, Alabama, in July of the same year.

His regiment fought at the first big battle at Perrygrove, Arkansas, and later in the siege and capture of Vicksburg and Fort Blakely, Alabama.

After his initial matriculation at Iowa State University in 1865, he entered the medical department at the University of Pennsylvania, from which he graduated in 1870. His interest in the eye led to an appointment at the Wills Eye Hospital in 1871.

Arthur Bedell recalled that Risley was a cordial gentleman who invited Bedell to his country home on the first day they met. Risley is described as a calm, quiet, dignified, and very gracious physician who was wholeheartedly sympathetic to his patients. His office routine was quite formal: when a patient entered, he was expected to place his calling card on a card plate, which was then taken to Dr. Risley's desk and the card placed in the order of receipt. If a patient had no card, his name and address were written on an 8 x 14-inch slate which was placed on the doctor's desk.

Risley worked in an unhurried manner and carried many new ideas to fruition, notably the Risley prism.

George E. deSchweinitz

George deSchweinitz, a consultant to Wills, was one of the truly great American ophthalmologists. Born in Philadelphia in 1858, he graduated with top honors in the class of 1881 at the University of Pennsylvania Medical School. He worked at Jefferson Medical

College as clinical professor of ophthalmology between 1892 and 1896; in 1896, he was made full professor. In 1901, he followed William Norris as professor at the University of Pennsylvania and worked there until his retirement in 1924. He was then appointed professor of ophthalmology in the graduate school of the University of Pennsylvania.

Dr. deSchweinitz was thoroughly devoted to the College of Physicians and served as its president between 1910 and 1912. He was also instrumental, with William Norris and Edward Jackson, in forming the Section of Ophthalmology in the College in 1893. His world renown in the field of ophthalmology became evident in 1923, when he was one of the first Americans invited to give the Bowman lecture.

T. B. Holloway and Frances Heed Adler

T. B. Holloway and Frances Heed Adler (Fig 4-4) were originally attending surgeons at Wills Eye Hospital before becoming heads of the department of ophthalmology at the University of Pennsylvania. Holloway served from 1924 to 1936, and Adler from 1933 to 1937. Adler initiated the residency program at the University. His first resident, Harold G. Scheie, succeeded him as chairman. The present head of ophthalmology, Myron Yanoff, also has Wills ties, having served a retina fellowship there after completion of his residency.

Edward Jackson

Edward Jackson, an attending surgeon at the Wills Eye Hospital from 1890 to 1898, rose to national fame as an ophthalmologist, although most of this fame developed after he left Philadelphia for Denver, Colorado (Fig 4-5). Nevertheless, Jackson did spend the first 44 years of his life in this area, and it was in the City of Brotherly Love that he first demonstrated talents to the ophthalmic community.

Jackson was born in West Chester County and was a member of the Society of Friends. When he later moved to Denver, he became affiliated with the Unitarian Church, but in 1939 he renewed his membership in the Friends Meeting when he returned to Philadelphia.

A graduate of Union College with a degree in engineering, he immediately decided on a career in medicine rather than in engineering

Fig 4-4. Francis Heed Adler.

and entered the University of Pennsylvania, from which he graduated in 1878. His interest in ophthalmology resulted partly from an attack of diphtheria that left him with multiple paralyses, including a paralysis of accommodation. He read Donders' monumental work on refraction from cover to cover.

He moved to Philadelphia, where he became associated with Drs. Harlan, Fox, Randall, Norris, Oliver and Risley. In 1888, he was made professor of ophthalmology at the Philadelphia Polyclinic School. He was instrumental in the formation of the section of ophthalmology at the College of Physicians and probably would have been content to remain in Philadelphia had his wife not developed tuberculosis in 1894. This precipitated his move to Denver with his wife, three sons, and two daughters. Despite the move, Mrs. Jackson died in 1896, and Jackson subsequently moved back to Philadelphia. However, he then became apprehensive that his children might have become infected with tuberculosis, so he once again returned to Denver.

While in Philadelphia, Jackson published 22 papers covering many subjects, mainly refraction. One of his most notable contributions was the cross cylinder, which is still an essential instrument for the refractionist today.

The experience and satisfaction that came from his contributions to the organization of the section of ophthalmology of the College of Physicians inspired him to help in the formation of the American Academy of Ophthalmology and Otolaryngology. He is remembered

Fig 4-5. Jackson's own ophthalmic problem, paralysis of his accommodation, inspired him to become an ophthalmologist and to establish two important institutions: the ophthalmology department at the College of Physicians and the American Academy of Ophthalmology and Otolaryngology.

for these efforts each year when the annual Jackson Memorial Lecture is given at the Academy meeting.

William Zentmayer

William Zentmayer was an extremely well liked and dedicated ophthalmologist. His father, Joseph, was an instrument worker and optician who invented and made many different types of microscopes and won several prizes both at home and abroad; he was also one of the

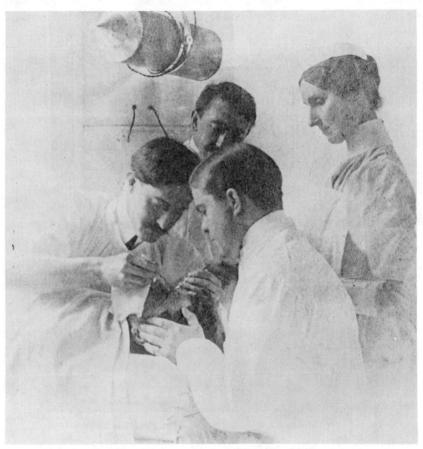

Fig 4-6. Homer Rhode, Harold Goldberg, Arthur Bedell, and Nurse Finley operating.

46

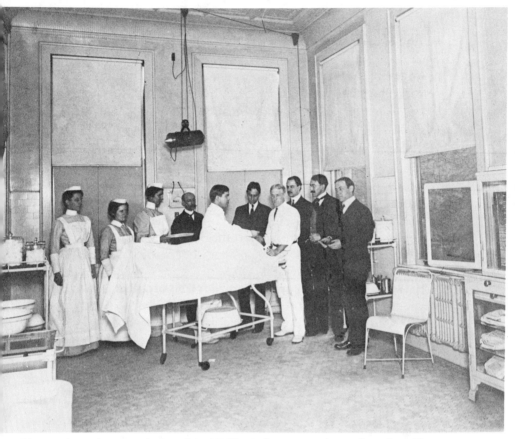

Fig 4-7. Operating room in the original Wills. A giant magnet hangs from the ceiling. Note the absence of surgical lights and surgical garb. A young Arthur Bedell stands near the patient's head.

first opticians to demand a prescription from the ophthalmologist before making spectacles.

Zentmayer graduated from the medical school of the University of Pennsylvania in 1887. In 1890, he was appointed assistant surgeon at the Wills Eye Hospital under the leadership of William Norris, and in 1901 he succeeded Norris as attending surgeon. He served in that position until 1928, when he retired at the age of 65.

Zentmayer was very active in the ophthalmic community. He was a fellow of the College of Physicians and served as chairman of the section of ophthalmology. In 1927, he served as president of the American Ophthalmological Society; he also served as chairman of the section of diseases of the eye, ear, nose, and throat of the State Medical Society.

An extremely knowledgeable and learned man, he was on the editorial board of the *Archives of Ophthalmology* and was editor of the *Transactions of the College of Physicians* from 1889 to 1930. He never married and truly devoted his life to the advancement of ophthalmology.

Arthur J. Bedell

Bedell was one of the most notable staff members that ever worked in Wills Eye Hospital (Figs 4-6 and 4-7). One of the first ophthalmologists to realize the importance of fundus photographs, he amassed a collection of thousands of kodachrome pictures over the years and gave these to Wills.

He was a robust man and is known for his arguments with Freddie Verhoeff of Boston and his faithful attendance at the Wills conferences, to which he often traveled by bus from Albany, New York, even at the age of 90. With his death in 1972, Wills lost its oldest living ex-resident. In many ways, his passing signified the end of an era.

Chapter 5

The Move to Spring Garden Street

Wills was growing fast and furiously when in 1873 there was an outbreak of contagious eye infection at the Wills Eye Hospital. Business came to an immediate halt, and a majority of the surgical staff refused to admit patients. About 44 fewer patients were admitted that year, and operations were postponed indefinitely. In the report for the year, the staff used this contagious outbreak to point to the need for better accommodations; in particular, they cited the fact that the infection was probably the result of poor ventilation and overcrowding in the wards. In addition, they said, the hospital had failed to keep pace with the increased population of the city; there had been no increase in the number of beds in the hospital since the structure was built 40 years earlier.

At that time, the population of Philadelphia was about 726,000, which was even larger than that of Berlin and Vienna, each of which had a population of about 600,000. However, both of the latter cities had 120 to 130 beds for eye patients, whereas Philadelphia could offer only 40 beds. Therefore, the committee agreed that two new wards should be built, and they sent out an appeal to the city's residents for funds.

These wards opened on October 11, 1875. Each had a capacity of 20 beds. It took another 29 years, until 1908, for a third floor and basement to be completed (Figs 5-1 through 5-3).

By 1923, a new era had begun. Mr. Stephen Wierzbicki was appointed superintendent to the hospital (Fig 5-4). He had previously been a warrant officer in the United States Navy, and he was very

Fig 5-1. The original Wills after addition of a third floor. Cars of the period included a Packard (far left), Lincoln (fourth from left), and Erskine (fifth from left). The others could not be identified.

Fig 5-2. The Wills on Logan Circle in 1931.

Fig 5-3. Logan Circle as it appears today. A hotel is planned for the site.

experienced in the administration of naval hospitals. The early 20th century brought more growth; in his report for 1928, Wierzbicki emphasized the marked increase in the number of patients admitted to the hospital compared with the number in former years. This was partly attributable to a reduction in the length of time patients stayed in the hospital; it dropped from 23 days in 1923 to 14 days in 1928 and to 12.06 days in 1930 (still a very long stay by today's standards). Therefore, Wierzbicki concluded, a considerable amount of additional space was needed.

Plans were made for an entirely new Wills, and in June 1930 the property on Logan Square was sold to Mr. Cyrus H.K. Curtis for $1,100,000 (Fig 5-5). It was understood that Mr. Curtis' purpose in acquiring the property was to erect a building in which musical

51

Fig 5-4. Stephen Wierzbicki, superintendent of Wills Eye.

programs could be held; unfortunately, this never came to pass. The old Wills Eye Hospital was used as a juvenile court from 1934 to 1938. It was not demolished until 1944. The permit for demolition was signed on December 30, 1943, at the request of Mary Curtis, and today the site is used as a parking lot (Fig 5-6), although an $80 million hotel complex is planned.

In March 1931 the Board of Directors of City Trusts, after analyzing growth patterns in the city, acquired ground on the northwest corner of Sixteenth and Spring Garden Streets and planned to build a new hospital at a cost of $290,000 (Fig 5-7). By the time the hospital was completed, however, it cost approximately $1,750,000. It was to be the largest hospital in the United States devoted to diseases of the eye.

The new site did not have the picturesque location of the old hospital, but it was felt to be convenient to both patients and staff because, at that time, Spring Garden Street was one of the most important thoroughfares of the city and was only two blocks from Broad Street. This made it accessible to traffic north, south, east, and west.

The lot was 197 feet by 170 feet and, was bordered on three sides by streets—Spring Garden Street on the south, Sixteenth Street on the east, and Brandywine Street on the north.

Mr. John Windrom, a well-known Philadelphia architect, was selected to design the new Wills Eye Hospital, which ultimately consisted of a basement, six floors, and a roof apartment for the

WILLS HOSPITAL
GIFT OF A GROCER

Site Cost $20,000 Long Ago, Now Cyrus H. K. Curtis Pays $1,100,000 for Part of It

---

MUSIC TEMPLE GOING THERE

In 1832 a hospital was established for the "relief of the indigent blind and lame" under the will of a philanthropic grocer, whose father had amassed a fortune from an original capital of $10.

The grocer was James Wills, Jr., whose father, as coachman to the eminent Anthony Benezet, had learned the lesson of philanthropy before he had means to give.

The hospital was the Wills Eye Hospital, which, after standing

Fig 5-5. The sale of Wills to Cyrus Curtis.

B. & B. FORM 14

"A" YARD SPACE APPROVED

DEPARTMENT MEMORANDUM

INSPECTOR.

	CLASS	MATERIAL	OCCUPANCY	LIVE LOAD
PRESENT BUILDING				
NEW BLDG. OR ADD.			*Tear down*	

PERMIT No. *3 2 7 4*

FEE. $

SURVEY VOUCHER No. _____ DIST. _____ DATE _____

PLAN NO. _____

Application for Permit for Additions, Alterations, Repairs, One-Story Structures, Frame Buildings, Bay Windows, Heaters, Boilers and Engine Foundations, Demolitions, etc.

Philadelphia, *December 30* 19 *43*

To the BUREAU OF BUILDING INSPECTION.

The undersigned applies for a permit to construct the following described work:

Give the exact location (street and number, or side of street and distance from nearest cross street.)

1810-24 _____ *Place 2* ____ *10* __ Ward.

What is the present building used for? _____

What will the new building or addition be used for? _____

Give definite particulars as to work proposed and materials used _____

Tear down + clear site

Fig 5-6. Mary Curtis signed the papers for the demolition of the Wills Eye Hospital on Logan Circle in 1943.

superintendent (Fig 5-8). John McShain constructed the 200-bed hospital, and it opened in November 1932 (Fig 5-8).

The roof apartment has an interesting story associated with it. Mr. Melvin Sutley, who succeeded Stephen Wierzbicki as superintendent of the hospital, held many séances in his apartment, particularly on Sunday nights. It was not uncommon for a resident on duty to see the best cuts of meats and the freshest vegetables being transported upstairs for the séances. Mr. Sutley was so convinced of his ability to communicate with the dead that he often spoke of his late wife in the present tense. Once, when leaving for Japan on a trip, he spoke in the plural, stating that "we will visit Tokyo. . . ." It was the day after his departure on this trip that a phone call came from his apartment. The caller obviously was in acute distress. When notified, the resident went to the emergency room to get a blood pressure cuff and stethoscope

54

and asked one of the nurses working there if she would accompany him
to Mr. Sutley's apartment. She was at first reluctant to go because of
the "communications with the dead" that reportedly took place there
but finally relented. A gentleman was found in the apartment with a
perforated diverticulum; he identified himself as the medium who ran
the séances. He was quickly transferred to Graduate Hospital, where,
happily, he made a speedy recovery.

The operating rooms were on the fourth floor and were easily
accessible from the elevators. At either end of the floor, there was an

SPRING GARDEN ST. FORGING AHEAD AS BUILDING LOCATION

Its Broad Expanse Makes Splendid Sites for Larger Structures

WILLS EYE HOSPITAL SOON TO BUILD THERE

By JOHN C. HARE

The recent purchase by the Wills
Eye Hospital of a plot of ground at
the northwest corner of 16th and
Spring Garden streets, as a site for
its new building, has called attention to the advantages of Spring
Garden street as a location for large
buildings, which find it necessary to
be located close to the central section. The price paid for the lot,
about $8 per square foot, cannot be
considered a high figure for frontage
on a street of the width of Spring

Fig 5-7. Plans to move to 16th and
Spring Garden.

55

Fig 5-8. The Wills at 16th and Spring Garden
Street opened in November 1932.

WILLS HOSPITAL OPENS AT NEW SITE

Century-Old Eye Institution Dedicates Structure at 16th and Spring Garden Sts.

MOST MODERN IN NATION

With the dedication today of the new building of the Wills Hospital at the northwest corner of 16th and Spring Garden sts., this city's reputation as a medical center will be further enhanced with the added distinction of now having the largest hospital in the country devoted to opthalmology.

The Wills Hospital, formerly known as the Wills Eye Hospital, moves into a carefully planned new home admirably equipped to carry on its century of useful work of curing or alleviating every form of

Fig 5-8. (*continued*).

open surgical ward, so that guests arriving to visit relatives would walk through the operating room suite. Not infrequently they peered through porthole windows in the operating room doors to catch a glimpse of the surgery taking place. Undoubtedly on more than one occasion someone looked in and, without realizing it, saw a relative or friend having a cataract removed.

This, fortunately, was remedied in the mid 1960s, when a new operating suite was constructed with all the latest equipment. It was isolated from the elevators, and unauthorized spectators were finally excluded from the surgical scene.

57

Chapter 6

Cataract Surgery at Wills

The Wills Eye Hospital has always been known for its cataract surgery and for the training in cataract surgery that its resident surgeons receive. The evolution of the cataract operation as practiced in the United States may be traced by examining the contributions Wills Eye staff members made to the cataract technique. Littel, Hays, Agnew, and Norris all described procedures that were popular in their time, and each recorded his opinions of the early methods.

When the hospital was first founded, three ways of operating were in vogue: couching, keratonyxis (or breaking up of the lens), and extraction. Various modifications have since been made to these three methods.

Couching, or depression, was the operation of the earliest surgeons and until the beginning of the 18th century was the only procedure practiced. It consisted of simply displacing the lens below the level of the pupil. It was easy to do and often gave immediate, successful results.

Keratonyxis was performed by tearing the capsule and fragmenting the lens so that the lens substance might be exposed to the action of the aqueous and thus be gradually dissolved and absorbed. This procedure was very popular, and advances were made in this procedure well up to the end of the 1800s. In Wharton Jones' book (edited by Isaac Hays), the following opinion was given:

> Considered as an operation, this is the most successful of all those of the cataract, both in performance and extent of injury necessarily inflicted upon the eye. . . . In the cases proper for the operation, the prognosis is

good. . . . In general, it may be said that in children the absorption process proceeds more quickly than in adults.

Littel also felt that this operation was particularly applicable to cataract in children, a fact we today know to be true. The instrument of choice was a needle, which in many cases, Littel pointed out, could not be well controlled by the surgeon, especially when it was introduced through the sclera, as it commonly was.

In 1745, Daviel revolutionized the operation for the cataract by making an incision into the eyeball and removing the opaque lens from the eye. Some years later, Beer of Vienna modified Daviel's method and invented a triangular knife by means of which a sufficiently large section of the cornea could be made to allow removal of the lens from the eye. No iridectomy was done. Many cases were successful, but unfortunately many were lost to infection; this was thought to be because the incision lay anteriorly on the cornea. Therefore, for some years a more peripheral incision was made in the sclera, though the results obtained with this modification were not much better than those with the corneal incision.

Littel was not in favor of extraction and criticized it while still advocating couching. In any event, the procedure was adopted by most staff members after von Graefe made modifications in the method of extraction in 1862. The first improvement suggested by von Graefe was a linear incision, which did away with the gaping caused by the Beer incision. Von Graefe made his incision in the upper part of the cornea and combined it with an iridectomy, another modification. About the same time, Jacobson introduced a flap section in the sclera, also combining it with an iridectomy.

By this time, the complications of subacute inflammation with couching and excessive length of time for absorption with keratonyxis had been pointed out by Agnew. By 1890, Norris again emphasized the complications of discissions and absorption. Agnew practiced von Graefe's method from the very start and was impressed with the results he obtained with it. Excellent as von Graefe's results were, however, he further improved them a few years later by introducing the modified flap operations, which combined the advantages of the linear incision, by which he obtained a closed coaptation of the lips of the wound, with those of a scleral incision. A narrow or linear knife was soon almost universally employed and is still used today.

Many modifications followed, including preliminary iridectomy, performed several weeks prior to lens extraction. The objections raised to this were a greater risk of infection in two operative procedures and the greater mental and physical strain experienced by the patient.

The methods of opening the capsule also differed, but the cystotome was preferred by most surgeons. Others tore off a bit of the capsule with forceps, while the more experienced and skillful operators incised the capsule with the tip of the cataract knife as the instrument was swept across the anterior section. Still others thought it was better to open the capsule and ripen the lens several days before completing the cataract operation. This approach, however, was never widely accepted.

From 1872 to 1891, about 1,428 cataract extractions were performed at Wills Eye Hospital. This represented 1.1% of the cases seen at the hospital. An interesting survey of cataract patients reported by Edward Jackson showed that 449 of 1,545 patients over the age of 50 were noted to have some lens opacities. Arranged in 5-year periods, the percentages were as follows: 15% between ages 50 and 55, 16.1% between 55 and 60, 30.2% between 60 and 65. In a 10-year period, in patients between the ages of 65 and 75, 77% were noted to have lens opacities.

Before the days of general anesthesia, even cocaine was not available. As a result, patients and surgeons had to make do as best they could, the one enduring pain and the other trying to operate skillfully and swiftly. After general anesthetics were introduced in the 1840s, the question arose as to whether the relief from pain they afforded the patient combined with the opportunity given the surgeon to operate with greater precision and ease counterbalanced the evils of retching and vomiting that the anesthetic often produced. One must remember that no sutures were used at this time, so that the vomiting could be a considerable problem. Interestingly enough, Agnew felt that it was better not to use anesthetic because, he said, the operation was not painful and a few words of assurance from the surgeon could put the patient at ease. One must conclude from this that Agnew himself probably never had a cataract operation. Still, in an interesting survey conducted by Derby in Boston, 100 patients were operated on while under an anesthetic and eight eyes were lost. A second group of 100 patients were operated on without the advantage of an anesthetic and only one eye was lost. Once again, however, had sutures been used, the results certainly would have been different.

In 1881, antiseptics were introduced in ocular surgery, and aseptic precautions were observed. Still, antisepsis was not the great boon to ophthalmology that it was to general surgery. Many of us can still remember the barehanded ophthalmic surgeon (even in the 1950s and early 1960s) and the low incidence of infection in their operations.

In 1884, Carl Koller discovered cocaine. This was a big help to the ophthalmic surgeon, as was the later introduction of Novocain. With the advent of local anesthetics, the number of cataract operations increased markedly. In 1880, at the Wills Eye Hospital, 262 extractions were done; by 1920, there were over 600 extractions, and by 1930, over 1,000.

In 1921, Colonel Henry Smith, who had gained much experience performing cataract operations in India, visited the Wills Eye Hospital. An Irishman trained in Britian, Smith served for years in India as an officer in the British Medical Service. Although only a general medical officer in charge of the health in the Punjab, he developed a particular interest in diseases of the eye, especially cataract.

His operative skill was well known throughout India. He averaged 3,000 cataract operations each year. Since he could not speak the various dialects, he was unable to communicate with his patients; as a result, he devised an operation that could be performed without the patient's cooperation, and thus the intracapsular method of extraction was developed. By the time he retired in 1921, Colonel Smith had performed 50,000 cataract operations, mostly by the intracapsular method.

Actually, the intracapsular method did not originate with Colonel Smith, and he never claimed that it did. The first surgeons to practice this method of extraction were Richter and Beer and, later, the Pagenstechers of Germany, who obtained excellent results with it. The Pagenstechers maintained their clinic in Wiesbaden as late as 1959. Smith, however, modified the operation and had far greater experience with it than did anyone else.

He visited the Wills Eye Hospital on November 17, 1921, and operated on 18 senile cataracts. His results were followed up by Dr. William Zentmayer and showed a corrected vision of 6/6 in two cases, 6/9 and 6/12 in two cases, 6/15 in three cases, 6/20 in four cases, and

6/30 in two cases. In one case, no follow-up was available. Vitreous loss and incarceration of the iris occurred in 38% of the patients, and in most there was residual haze.

Although Smith's results in this country were somewhat disastrous, it was the general opinion that he was operating at considerable disadvantage. His assistants were unknown to him and the surroundings were strange; also, large crowds watched him operate, which no doubt had an effect. Still, all those who witnessed his surgery admired his skill, poise, and command of the situation.

While operating in India for hours at a stretch, the Colonel had grown accustomed to smoking during the operation. He usually smoked cigars and lighted up before scrubbing. The cigar then remained in his mouth until the operation was almost completed. While smoking his customary cigar during surgery at Wills, one of the observers became concerned that the ash from the cigar would fall into the eye of the patient and actually felt compelled to draw attention to this. He said to Smith: "Pardon me, Colonel, but aren't you afraid that an ash from your cigar is going to fall into the patient's eye?" Smith replied quickly and with certainty: "It never has yet."

Although all admired the skill he demonstrated at Wills Eye Hospital, there were those who felt that he would be better named "Vitreous Smith" rather than "Indian Smith," the name that had been given to him because of his long service in the subcontinent.

Through the years, intracapsular cataract extraction has become well accepted and is the operation performed most often today. However, innovations have evolved over the years, and Wills Eye Hospital has contributed to many. Probably one of the most significant contributions to cataract surgery has been the use of the cryoprobe for extraction of the lens, a procedure devised by an ex-resident of the Wills Eye Hospital, Dr. Charles Kelman, who served his residency from 1958 to 1960. There is no corner of the world where cataract extraction is performed without the aid of the cryoprobe.

Kelman also developed the technique of phacoemulsification, a method of fragmenting the lens with an ultrasonic tip. This is a procedure done under the operating microscope and requires the most skilled of surgeons. It has been controversial but is now widely accepted. Thus, two significant present-day innovations of cataract surgery are attributable to a Wills Eye Hospital ex-resident.

Wills Eye Hospital also pioneered another popular modern addition to cataract surgery, the introduction of an intraocular lens into the eye to replace the removed cataractous one. Though highly controversial, it is being used extensively.

The first intraocular lenses were devised in England by Professor Ridley, who started the procedure in 1949. His work came to the attention of Dr. Warren Reese, an attending surgeon at Wills Eye, who began to correspond with Ridley. Ultimately, Dr. Reese performed 300 intraocular Ridley lenses between 1952 and 1956. This far exceeded the 77 that Ridley himself had inserted.

The first report by Reese on intraocular lenses concerned 20 cases. All had good results. Dr. Reese had wanted to perform his first Ridley implant without a crowd, so he inserted the first one 4 days before the annual clinical conference in 1952. Having performed one, he then did another during the Wills Eye Conference.

Reeese performed the intraocular lens operation before he actually met Ridley, who lived in a cottage in Wilshire, England. While driving in his car, Reese first glimpsed Ridley standing midstream in hip waders, intent upon fishing, and Dr. Reese still fondly recalls this memory, which marked the beginning of a long friendship. The two became very close and visited each other often.

As the only surgeon in the United States who had experience with Ridley's procedure. Dr. Reese discussed Ridley's first paper given at the Academy Meeting in Chicago. A short time later, under Reese's tutelage, Dr. Turgut Hamdi began inserting Ridley implants and newer implants as they were developed. Certainly there is no one in the United States who has a longer follow-up of intraocular lenses than Dr. Hamdi, whose experience goes back well over 25 years, a record no other implanter can equal.

Another close friend of Reese's was Cecil O'Brien. He was an excellent ophthalmologist, in many ways best known for his out-spokenness as well as his intellect. He started his career at the Wills Eye Hospital, but, restless for the open spaces of the western frontier, he packed his bags and moved to the Midwest. He there became chairman of the University of Iowa Eye Department, where subsequently he taught our present ophthalmologist-in-chief, Tom Duane.

O'Brien used to teasingly accuse Reese of being afraid to visit him in the West for fear of being attacked by Indians. Reese denied the allegation and proved his fearlessness by arriving some months later on the train. To his surprise, O'Brien and his residents were waiting on the station platform dressed as Indians.

As already mentioned, O'Brien was a person who said what was on his mind. As a resident, he once watched Dr. William Zentmayer examine a young man. To relax the patient, Zentmayer asked what the young man did for a living. The answer was that he was a bricklayer. A few seconds later Zentmayer inquired again as to the patient's occupation, and the reply was again "bricklayer." Then as Zentmayer shifted to look in the second eye, he asked the same question a third time, but before he could finish, O'Brien said quietly from the doorway, "He's still a bricklayer, Doctor!"

Other cataract surgeons at Wills who were excellent technicians included Dr. Posey, who operated expeditiously, and Drs. William Zentmayer and Frank Parker, who are renowned for making cataract incisions and iridectomies at the same time with the von Graefe knife. More recently, Dr. Edmund Spaeth performed numerous cataract operations, as did Dr. James Shipman, both of whom developed national reputations as ophthalmic surgeons. Dr. Spaeth was also noted for his work in motility and for his abilities as a teacher.

In any discussion of cataract extraction, one can not fail to mention the exceptional talent of P. Robb McDonald. His technical skill was matched by incomparable clinical judgment and an ability to keep pace with rapid changes in surgical technique. Because of his exceptional abilities, other cataract surgeons began to send their complications to him, and he became an authority in this field.

Chapter 7

The Organization of Wills Eye Hospital

From the 1930s to the 1960s, Wills Eye Hospital was organized around several general eye services, each of which was headed by a chief. There were three clinic areas in the hospital, and each patient was examined by members of the staff as well as by one resident from each clinic. For example, the Tassman Service would see patients and operate on Monday and Thursday, the Leopold Service would see patients Tuesday and Friday, and the Spaeth Service would see patients on Wednesday and Saturday. After the external examination, patients were sent to a dark room for dilation and examination (usually with the direct ophthalmoscope) of the ocular fundus (Fig 7-1). They later had to return on a different day for refraction.

Each service chief and his lieutenant were responsible for one of the clinic rooms and the surgery generated from the clinic 2 days each week. The result was that some of the staff would be responsible for manning the clinics, while others would be in the operating room assisting residents with surgery. Each private physician would also operate on his private patients on those days.

By the late 1950s, one of the busiest chiefs was Irving Leopold (Fig 7-2), who was instrumental in bringing about organizational changes. By this time, too, several offers came to Dr. Irving Leopold from other institutions. To counter these, the Board of City Trusts and the Board of Surgeons voted to make Leopold the overall chief with the idea of bringing together many of the potentially excellent functions and services at the Wills Hospital (Fig 7-3). One of the first accomplishments of this new regime was to decrease the number of

Fig 7-1. General receiving clinic, 16th and Spring Garden Streets, in the 1950s.

chiefs from nine to five. Instead of there being three services a day, each one performing twice a week, they were reduced to five, one for each of the working days of the week, and Saturdays became a teaching day, with use of the emergency room to handle the patients who could not come to the regular clinic during the week.

With Leopold as ophthalmologist-in-chief, specialty clinics in glaucoma, uveitis, and external disease were begun. Pediatric ophthalmology, which was supported by a grant from the National Council to Combat Blindness, was successful from the onset. Other subspecialty services were also started and are described in Chapter 9.

It also became apparent that it would be advisable for the Wills Hospital to have a medical school affiliation. Actually, Wills already

Fig 7-2. Jack Matthews and Irving Leopold leaving Wills Hospital.

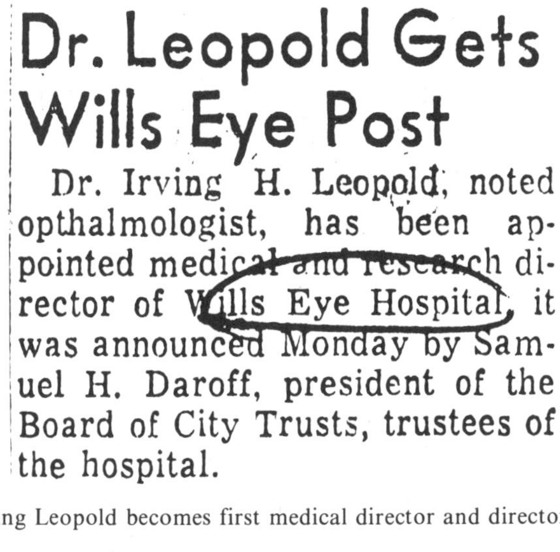

Dr. Leopold Gets Wills Eye Post

Dr. Irving H. Leopold, noted opthalmologist, has been appointed medical and research director of Wills Eye Hospital, it was announced Monday by Samuel H. Daroff, president of the Board of City Trusts, trustees of the hospital.

Fig 7-3. Irving Leopold becomes first medical director and director of research.

had a loose connection with the University of Pennsylvania because Leopold was then professor and chairman of the department of ophthalmology in the graduate school of medicine at the University of Pennsylvania as well as head of Wills. The majority of the residents at that time were participating in the University formal course prior to coming to Wills as residents. Still, there were some ophthalmologists who felt that because the Wills Eye Hospital was not part of a university, it could not have a department quite as good as that found in a university. To make sure that Wills Eye Hospital was not losing stature and national and international prestige, the administration began looking for a firmer association with a medical school. Leopold organized a committee which approached the University of Pennsylvania Medical School, Thomas Jefferson, Temple, and Hahnemann. Each was asked to think about forming an association with the Wills Hospital. However, it took a number of years to resolve this situation. Ultimately, Leopold left for New York, and it had not yet been decided which institution would be associated with Wills. However, the groundwork was laid for the next chief, Arthur Keeney, and his group to consummate an affiliation.

Under the leadership of Arthur H. Keeney (Fig 7-4), who was appointed in 1964, the inefficiency of seeing patients and having them come back later to the refraction clinic became apparent. Therefore, "one-stop" ophthalmic care developed. The clinic system was revamped, and better-equipped individual examining rooms were designed and built. This has made for better patient/doctor relationships and more pleasant surroundings for the patients.

Keeney also carried on the quest for a university affiliation. This culuminated in a marriage to Temple University, with the hope that a new Wills Hospital would be built at the North Broad Street Medical Complex. State funds never became available, however, and ultimately the association was dissolved.

Negotiations then began with the University of Pennsylvania and Jefferson. On July 20, 1972, Wills and Jefferson did affiliate, and the new hospital and a single residency program are fruits of that union.

In the 1950s and 1960s the chiefs were Drs. Wilfred Fry, Patrick J. Kennedy, Irving H. Leopold, P. Robb McDonald, Robert Mulberger, James Shipman, Edmund B. Spaeth, and Isaac Tassman. All contributed much to the modernization of Wills Eye Hospital.

Dr. A. Keeney
To Supervise at
Wills Hospital

The appointment of Dr. Arthur Hail Keeney, associate professor of Opthalmology at the University of Louisville School of Medicine, to supervise the medical and training activities of the Wills

Fig 7-4. Arthur Keeney succeeds Irving Leopold as Ophthalmologist-in-chief, November 1964.

Known as "Mr. Wills," Shipman acquired a significant reputation for his skill as a surgeon. He was one of the first surgeons at Wills Eye Hospital to do corneal transplants with a two-blade knife and also did much to popularize the intracapsular cataract extraction in Philadelphia.

Shipman was also a local pioneer in retinal detachment surgery. Often after a person had a retinal detachment, the eye was lost. Bed rest was stressed for several weeks before and after surgery, and results were not what they are today. In his memory, there is a Shipman Memorial Fund, which is used to pay for a research retina fellowship.

P. Robb McDonald (Fig 7-5) and Patrick Kennedy followed Shipman as pioneers in retinal detachment surgery. Quickly McDonald recognized the value of the work of Charles Schepens of Boston. Schepens developed and popularized the binocular indirect ophthalmoscope as a practical instrument to be worn on the head so that the surgeon could perform indirect ophthalmoscopy using scleral depression. This, as it turned out, was a major breakthrough in the cure of retinal detachment because the retina could now be adequately examined. Wills Eye Hospital thus became an early proponent of the new techniques of retinal detachment surgery, especially the use of a polyethylene tube to encircle the globe during retinal detachment surgery. This, however, was a rigid material that led to many cases of

Fig 7-5. The inestimable P. Robb McDonald.

intrusion. As an alternative material, McDonald suggested to Schepens that he try silicone rubber instead, and this is still the material of choice today.

Two other chiefs active from the 1940s through the 1960s were E. B. Spaeth and I. S. Tassman. In addition to their contribution to Wills, both sired sons who have followed in their tradition at Wills: Philip G. Spaeth, George L. Spaeth, and William Tasman.

Edmund Spaeth was noted for his ophthalmic surgery, particularly in the fields of plastics and motility, and his textbook of *Ophthalmic Surgery* was the classic of its day.

One interesting anecdote reported by the late Dr. Ned Shaw concerns a lecture on the cranial nerves given by Dr. Spaeth at the graduate school of medicine at the University of Pennsylvania. There was, as usual, a large audience. Dr. Spaeth, a natural actor, arrived with a fresh brain. He demonstrated to the class the olfactory nerve, optic nerve, and oculomotor nerve. When he came to the trochlear nerve, he had some difficulty finding it and finally, with frustrated gusto, said "The dickens with it!" With that, he crushed the brain in his left hand, placed it back on the tray, and proceeded to draw the nerves on the blackboard.

Often the apple does not fall far from the tree. This story is much like one concerning his sons, Phil, Karl, and George, at a baseball game at Philadelphia's Old Shibe Park. Their seats were in front of some obnoxious fans who kept dropping their lunch. No one said anything until an apple accidentally fell in Phil's lap. Phil picked up the apple and said: "Excuse me, is this yours?" As he asked the question, Phil crushed the apple and dropped the remains in the lap of the fan behind. From that point on there was no problem.

Tassman was noted for his expertise in medical diseases affecting the eye and refraction and was the first chief of refraction at the Wills Eye Hospital. His book on *Eye Manifestation of Internal Diseases* went through three editions and was a standard text of the day in Europe as well as in the United States. He was also the first to devise a physiologic glue for corneal lacerations, on which he first reported at the second annual Wills Eye Conference (Fig 7-6), and he directed the Wills Eye Conference as chairman of the conference committee through the 1950s and into the 1960s.

71

Blood 'Cement' in Eye Surgery Replaces Stitches, Helps Grafts

The successful use of a blood "cement" in place of stitches in certain eye operations was reported today at an annual clinical conference at Wills Eye Hospital.

The report was made by Dr. I. S. Tassman, associate professor of opthrthalmology at the Graduate School of Medicine of the University of Pennsylvania.

Dr. Tassman said he has used the technique at Wills Hospital for about a year in some 250 operations. These mostly have been cataract also promotes it growing into the eye.

Components of the patient's own blood usually are used in the technique, Dr. Tassman continued. He pointed out it was originally used in skin grafting.

Thrombin Added

He said that a single drop of blood plasma to which several drops of thrombin, a factor of the blood, are added suffice to form the "cement" for a corneal graft. It re-

Fig 7-6. Description of the first physiologic glue.

Chapter 8

The Residency Program

Wills Eye Hospital has always been interested in, and actively involved in, the teaching and training of ophthalmologists. As early as 1839, Isaac Parrish began a course of lectures in the hospital which were continued until his death in 1852. Other members of the staff were also active in demonstrating cases to visiting physicians and students. By 1867, the Board passed a bylaw that lecturing and teaching should be continued.

During this period, it was the custom for students of the University of Pennsylvania and the Jefferson Medical School to attend clinics at Wills Eye Hospital, where their education in diseases of the eye was acquired. In Philadelphia, no regular courses of lectures on diseases of the eye were given in medical schools until 1870. That year, the department of ophthalmology was started at the University of Pennsylvania and was followed 24 years later by the department at the Jefferson Hospital. Although the chair of ophthalmology at Jefferson was not founded until 1894, lectures had been given by Dr. Thompson for a number of years before establishment of a department.

Advertisements in 1873 in the *American Journal of the Medical Sciences* by Dr. Hall of the staff at Wills Eye Hospital and Drs. Levis and Dyer made known the fact that courses in ophthalmology were given at the Wills Eye Hospital. Dr. McClure, who initiated the lectures, had recently returned from studying abroad. His evening lectures at the Wills Eye Hospital illustrated various phases of the dioptric system of the eye, utilizing lantern slides that he had made himself. These lectures proved to be very popular, but their success created some jealousy among his peers.

It is difficult to pinpoint the exact time when official residency programs started at the Wills Eye Hospital, but the earliest listed ex-resident is John Neill in 1839. Certainly the residency program was firmly in operation by the early 1900s.

The minutes of the hospital meeting on November 4, 1912, reveal the emerging hierarchy of the hospital. The Board of Directors recommended that white uniforms be worn by the staff and that they should have the following insignia: surgeons, four ½-inch stripes on the sleeves; assistant surgeons, one ½-inch stripe and one ¼-inch stripe; house surgeons, two ¼-inch stripes; and clinical assistants, no stripe at all. They also recommended that a white apron be provided to cover the knees of the surgeons and assistant surgeons when they were treating cases in the clinic. A broad cape, which could be sterilized, was ordered for visitors in the operating rooms, and operating gowns were furnished for assistant surgeons and their assistants.

During the early 1900s, it was mandatory that the junior resident physicians and a junior nurse assist in operations and make visits in the wards as emergencies arose. As of 1911 and 1912, the resident physician served for 1 year, beginning January 1. During this period, there were two residents, a junior resident and a senior resident. However, by 1912 the work load was increasing at the hospital and a request for a third resident was made. It was also suggested that a committee consisting of three members of the staff be selected by the president of the staff to examine future applicants for the position of resident surgeon at the hospital. The committee was then to report to the Board of Surgeons "the general fitness of the gentleman making application for the position."

Clinical training at the Wills Eye Hospital has always been excellent; its quality did not change through the transition of the move from Logan Square to Spring Garden Street. In this period, the number of residents gradually increased, as did the length of time served in the residency. From 1 year it was increased to 18 months, and this was the requisite time until May 1947, when the committee on residents submitted a plan for increasing the resident service from 18 months to 2 years. This, they felt, would afford an additional 2 weeks on each service and would therefore upgrade the training.

The residency committee was given the responsibility of looking into the credentials of applicants for residency appointments. After an adequate number had been screened from the total number of applicants, a smaller number was selected and invited to appear before the Board of Attending Surgeons at their January meeting for further examination and recommendation to the Board of City Trusts for appointment as residents. Many tales of these interviews have filtered down through the years. Applicants frequently stood around the perimeter of the boardroom, which at that time was on the Brandywine Street side of the first floor of the hospital; each wore a tag attached to his lapel, stating his name. There were at that time nine chiefs, and each of them moved around the room asking whatever question he so desired of each applicant. Frequently this *modus operandi* of interviewing curdled the stomachs of even the most hearty.

One cannot forget, as well, how in the 1950s Dr. Wilfred Fry spent a good deal of his time selecting residents. Often he was seen interviewing them on the pew-type benches that were then present in the lobby. Usually two other members were on the committee with Dr. Fry. Two who served in this capacity were Drs. William Annesley and Philip Spaeth, but as the latter two tell it, most of the decisions were actually made on the benches in the lobby, and their job was to ratify the selections.

During this period, residents entered every 3 months. This was an approach with many hazards, the most significant of which was that if the resident 3 months ahead of you was a turkey, your stay at Wills could be most unhappy. This system also allowed for each resident to eventually become the chief resident for the last 3 months of his tenure and was climaxed with farewell parties given by many of the staff men, including Drs. Shipman, Spaeth, Tassman, and Kennedy.

The practice of taking on a new resident every 3 months was finally abolished in favor of having a class start each July 1. This process was in effect by the late 1950s, and at that time seven residents were taken in each group, so that there was a total of 14 in the 2-year class. By 1958, it was decided that one of the senior residents should be designated as the chief resident. The first to have this honor was Dr. Ralph Hamilton, who now practices in Memphis, Tennessee. He was succeeded by Dr. Jerome Montana in 1959. This practice continues today.

Up until this time, it had been a prerequisite for a resident at Wills

Eye Hospital to have had a basic course in ophthalmology before entering the training program. Several courses were given, the most notable of which was at the graduate school of the University of Pennsylvania, headed at one time by William Shoemaker, Edmund Spaeth, and Irving Leopold. Many of the men who taught at the graduate school were members of the staff of Wills, as evidenced by Figure 8-1, which shows the faculty at the graduate school of the University of Pennsylvania in 1937.

In 1965, the length of the residency increased to 3 years, and a new class of seven residents was selected. By then, too, Arthur H. Keeney had accepted the position of ophthalmologist-in-chief at Wills Eye, and under his guidance a basic science course given by staff members of the

Dean Meeker
Vice Dean Shoemaker
Prof. Zentmayer
Dr. Branfield (pres.)
Prof. Peters
Prof. Langdon
Dr. Easley (sec)
Dr. Henry

9. Dr. Conahan
10. Prof. Batson
11. Dr. Shipman
12. Dr. Tassman
13. Dr. Reese
14. Dr. Spaeth
15. Dr. Charles
16. Dr. Rudolphy

17. Dr. Fewell
18. Dr. Smalens
19. Dr. Gifford
20. Dr. Dies
Esterly
22. Dr. Mengel
23. Dr. Kelly
24. Dr. Fry

25. Dr. Muir
26. Dr. Shuster
27. Dr. Kaufman
28. Dr. Wells
29. Dr. Wright
30. Dr. Earnshaw

31. Prof. De Renyi
32. Dr. Dattner
33. Dr. Kennedy
34. Dr. Loutfallah
35. Dr. Smith
36. Dr. Goldcamp
37. Dr. Jacquot
38. Dr. Gunderson

CLASS of OPHTHALMOLOGY

Fig 8-1. 1937 faculty and class of ophthalmology, graduate school of medicine, University of Pennsylvania.

hospital was held on the premises. This course was much shorter than the 9-month course at the graduate school of the University of Pennsylvania and covered only the most basic aspects of ophthalmology. Daily lectures given throughout the remainder of the year covered the fine points. This policy has worked well since its inception and is currently contnued at Wills Eye, except that in addition to our own first-year residents, we now have first-year residents from other institutions as well, notably from Temple University, Jefferson Hospital (which is now, of course, part of the Wills Eye program), and South Carolina.

The number of residents gradually increased until it reached an all-time high of 44. This was felt to be an excessive number, and gradually it was cut back to between 30 and 32.

As the affiliation with Jefferson Medical College evolved, it became necessary to integrate the separate residency program at Jefferson with the one at Wills. Now, for the first time, a unified class has been selected, to begin July 1980. Twelve residents will be in that class and will represent what was previously two separate residency programs.

The prestige of Wills over the past years has continued to grow, and at the present time the training program offered here is one of the best in the country. This has been reflected in the growing number of applicants and the caliber of those applicants. For the class selected to begin in 1980, over 150 applications were received for 12 places. For the 1981 class, the number is up to 217. Of the 150 in the 1980 group, about 77 were interviewed and 12 were selected. The 1980 class was the first selected by a matching program. This step was long overdue and works to the advantage of both the candidate and the institution. Most important, however, it prevents one institution from trying to lure an exceptional candidate into its program before he/she has been interviewed elsewhere.

As additional evidence of the desirability of the program at Wills, it is important to point out that of 12 residents selected in 1979, Wills matched five of its first six choices. It was necessary to go only to our 19th choice to fill 12 slots, compared to an average of 30 choices to fill 10 places at other institutions.

In the future, as the Wills affiliation with Jefferson grows, there will be additional changes made in the residency program. The new hospital and the merger are no doubt steps in the evolution of more-advanced ways to train ophthalmologists.

Subspecialty Services and Fellowships

By the late 1950s, newer techniques in retinal detachment surgery were developed, mostly because of the ingenuity and perseverance of Dr. Charles Schepens in Boston. As mentioned earlier, his development of the binocular indirect ophthalmoscope as a practical instrument was a major breakthrough in the treatment of retinal detachment, one obtained against great odds and criticism. Ultimately, of course, his theories and preachings were proved correct. We at Wills were fortunate that Dr. P. Robb McDonald saw the wisdom of Dr. Schepens' teachings.

Under McDonald's direction, indirect ophthalmoscopy came into its own at Wills Eye, and one of the early proponents was his first retinal fellow, L. K. Sarin. By 1961, residents were learning the use of indirect ophthalmoscopy, and it became apparent that there were areas in ophthalmology that might be better handled by subspecialization. As a result, fellowship programs began to proliferate around the country, initially in retina, cornea, glaucoma, and oculoplastics. From this evolved the subspecialty or vertical service with its own director(s) and staff.

Accordingly, at Wills the subspecialty services of retina, cornea, glaucoma, pediatric ophthalmology, oculoplastics, and neuroophthalmology were initiated, and each of these now offers much-sought-after fellowships. Thus, the postgraduate experience at Wills Eye Hospital rivals resident training in quality. In all, there are 12 or more postgraduate fellows subspecializing each year.

In many ways it is flattering that Wills Eye attracts the good fellows that it does, because those who have completed their training in ophthalmology and seek further specialty training presumably look very critically at the program they choose.

Coincident with the emergence of subspecialty services over the years, in 1979 the general receiving services became consolidated into one general receiving service, currently headed by seven chiefs.

Chapter 10

The Wills Eye Hospital Society and the Annual Clinical Conference

We cannot discuss the Wills Eye Hospital Society without relating it to the clinical conference, which has been a yearly mainstay of the functions associated with Wills. In 1927, the Wills Eye Hospital Society was organized, holding its first meeting on May 14. Originally the Society was a purely social organization formed to maintain friendly relations among the ex-residents and to renew their interest in the affairs of the hospital. It is a tribute to the Society that through the years its interest in Wills has never waned. The Society has met regularly for many years.

In 1947, the idea of holding an annual scientific meeting for 1 or 2 days was initiated. A committee was appointed to investigate the possibilities of such a meeting to be conducted by the staff, with one or more guest lectures, one of them to be the Bedell Lecture. A committee for investigation and further elaboration of this idea was appointed and included Dr. Carroll Mullen as chairman and Drs. Tassman and Fry as members of the committee. Thus, the record documents the birth of the annual clinical conference as October 1947.

At the meeting of the Board of Attending Surgeons on November 26, 1947, the special committee on the annual residents meeting gave a report. It brought forth the idea of a 2-day ex-residents scientific meeting, the first one to be held in the spring of 1949. It was also thought wise to hold a meeting of the Wills Society at the time; a guest lecturer would deliver the Bedell Lecture and there would be one or two other guest speakers, but presentations would be from the Wills Eye staff.

By the time of the spring meeting, plans had been almost finalized. It was agreed that invitations for a 2-day meeting would be sent to ophthalmologists throughout the United States, but especially to those in the eastern states. The only expenses would be those of sending the invitations and of renting any projection equipment that the hospital did not already have. The matter of housing and feeding guests would not be assumed by the hospital staff or management.

Tentative dates for the first clinical conference were Friday and Saturday, April 28 and 29, 1949. The program included a keynote address by a guest ophthalmologist, followed by the Bedell Lecture on Friday evening, April 28, at 8 PM. On Saturday, scientific lectures were to be given from 10 AM until 5 PM.

As an addendum to the plans for the meeting, it was resolved that the Board of Directors of City Trusts invite Professor Adelbert Fuchs to donate and permanently deposit at the Wills Eye Hospital the collection of correspondence and reprints from the estate of his father, Hofrat Professor Ernst Fuchs; if this invitation were accepted the collection should be assembled for exhibition at the meeting to be held in the spring of 1949. The son of Professor Fuchs was also to be an invited guest and was asked to speak on the life of his father and the contents of his collection.

Ultimately, the meeting took place on May 6 and 7, 1949, and Dr. Arthur J. Bedell was selected to deliver the first annual Bedell Lecture. Dr. Cecil S. O'Brien of the University of Iowa, a former celebrated resident at the Wills Eye Hospital, was invited to be another guest lecturer at the session. The remainder of the program was to include papers by I. S. Tassman, J. Shipman, L. Lehrfeld, W. Fry, I. Leopold, J. McGavic, B. Gettes, J. Klauder, and E. Spaeth (Fig 10-1).

As part of the program, each day during the noon recess, selected surgical cases were assigned to all operating rooms so that those who wished would have an opportunity to observe the ocular surgery of their choice (Fig 10-2). The conference concluded at 3 PM on Saturday, May 7, 1949, and was followed that evening by the annual dinner of the Wills Society. About 200 guests were expected to attend the meeting.

A total of 13 papers were read during the 2-day session, which included three half-day and one evening session, when the Bedell Lecture was given. In addition, each afternoon was devoted to a

81

THE STAFF AND EX-RESIDENTS

OF

THE WILLS HOSPITAL

EXTEND TO YOU A CORDIAL INVITATION

TO PARTICIPATE IN

A CLINICAL CONFERENCE

AT THE HOSPITAL

16TH AND SPRING GARDEN STREETS

PHILADELPHIA

MAY 6 AND 7, 1949

Fig 10-1. Program from first annual clinical conference.

The Wills Eye Hospital Society and the Annual Clinical Conference

Friday, May 6, 9:30 a.m.

DR. CARROLL R. MULLEN — *Presiding*

Dibutyline Sulfate, a Comparative Study of Its Cycloplegic Effects.
DR. BERNARD C. GETTES

Study of End Results of Glaucoma at the Wills Hospital.
DR. LOUIS LEHRFELD

Further Studies of the Chemical and Immunilogical Properties of Human Tears
DR. IRVING H. LEOPOLD

Diagnosis of Syphilitic Primary Optic Atrophy in the Pre-atrophic Stage
DR. JOSEPH V. KLAUDER *and* DR. GEORGE P. MEYER

—————

Luncheon — 1:00 p.m.

—————

Friday Afternoon, 2:00 p.m.

DR. WM. J. HARRISON — *Presiding*

A Follow-up Concerning Basket Implants
DR. WILFRED E. FRY

Experimental Studies with Physiologic Glue (Autogenous Plasma plus
Thrombin) For Use in the Eyes
DR. ISAAC S. TASSMAN

Causes of Failure in the Surgical Treatment of Glaucoma
DR. JOHN S. McGAVIC

Some Practical Facts Regarding Retinal Surgery With a Report of Results
in More Than Four Hundred Unselected and Consecutive Cases
DR. JAMES S. SHIPMAN

Fig 10-1. (*continued*).

Friday Evening, 8:15 p.m.

DR. WARREN S. REESE — *Presiding*

The Destruction of the Macula, Commonly Called Coloboma
DR. ARTHUR J. BEDELL

Saturday, May 7, 9:30 a.m.

DR. P. ROBB McDONALD — *Presiding*

Clinical Pathological Presentation
DR. JAMES H. PARKER

The Optics of Cylinder Magnification
DR. JOSEPH W. HALLETT

The Surgical Correction of Ptosis, Congenital and Acquired,
When Complicated by Other Oculomotor Situations.
DR. EDMUND B. SPAETH
Paper — Title to be announced
DR. CECIL O'BRIEN

Luncheon — 1:00 p.m.

Saturday Afternoon, 2:00 p.m.

OPERATIVE SURGERY

Fig 10-1. (*continued*).

selected eye operation. A total of 226 ophthalmologists registered for the conference, representing the following states and countries: California, Connecticut, Cuba, Delaware, District of Columbia, Florida, Georgia, Idaho, Indiana, Iowa, Kansas, Kentucky, Louisiana, Maine, Maryland, Massachusetts, Michigan, Nebraska, New Jersey, New York, North Carolina, Ohio, Pennsylvania, South

Carolina, Utah, Virginia, Washington, West Virginia, Wisconsin, and the Dominican Republic.

The meeting was a great success, and the conference committee recommended that this be an annual affair and that the Board of Attending Surgeons request permission from the Board of City Trusts to repeat this conference sometime in March 1950. As we all know, the Board acceded to this request and the conference has continued

Eye Specialists
See Rare Surgery

The first annual, two-day clinical conference of more than 200 of the Nation's leading eye specialists at Wills Hospital, 16th and Spring Garden sts., closed yesterday afternoon with a series of unusual operations.

The operations, performed by outstanding surgeons, included the insertion of a new-type "implant," a plastic and metal-mesh appliance to which eye muscles are sutured to enable a patient to move an artificial eye in a natural manner.

DAMAGED RETINA 'SEALED'

The delegates a l s o watched a corneal transplant, in which part of the cornea of a recently removed eye replaces the damaged area of a patient's eye, and a retinal detach-

Fig 10-2. Live surgery was a feature of the early conferences.

without interruption since 1949. The 1980 conference, which marks the opening of the third Wills Eye Hospital, represents the 32nd consecutive annual clinical conference.

Today, this conference draws over 700 guests per year and is one of the largest regional eye meetings in the United States. Without question, the Bedell lecturers are a "Who's Who" in ophthalmology (Appendix I). The success of this annual meeting and its growth are the result of the work of the indomitable chairmen, all of whom have made significant individual contributions. Those who have headed the annual clinical conference include Drs. Carroll Mullen, Isaac S. Tassman, Patrick J. Kennedy, Harold Barnshaw, Albert Cleveland, Robert Mulberger, Gerald Shannon, and Oram Kline.

The annual clinical conference continues to be deeply intertwined with the Ex-Residents Society of the Wills Eye Hospital. The majority of papers given at the conference are given by ex-residents, residents currently in training at Wills, and, now, fellows.

Since 1962, the Society has presented a silver tray to a member of the Wills family who has contributed significantly to the life of the hospital. The presentation is made during the conference and those so honored include Drs. James Shipman, James Delaney, Edmund Spaeth, Isaac Tassman, Wilfred Fry, Warren Reese, Patrick J. Kennedy, P. Robb McDonald, Kelvin Kasper, Harold Barnshaw, Albert Cleveland, James Shannon Jordan, Robert Mulberger, Robert E. Shoemaker, Arthur Keeney, and Joseph Hallett and Mr. Curtis Pritchard.

The interest and contributions of the Ex-Residents Society of the Wills Eye Hospital have, I believe, no equal. Probably no alumni group could maintain a stronger and more fervent interest in the institution from which they receive their training. At no other time was this more apparent than when the Ex-Residents Society pitched in during a difficult period when it appeared that we were headed for condominium status within the Jefferson complex. Spearheaded by Dr. Hunter Stokes, who at that time was president of the Ex-Residents Society, the plan was changed to the satisfaction of both institutions by the good offices of the Board of City Trusts and the administration of Jefferson Hospital. Thus, it is in large part because of the efforts of the Ex-Residents Society that we are presently located in a beautiful, free-standing eye hospital within the Jefferson complex on the corner of Ninth and Walnut Streets in center-city Philadelphia.

Chapter 11

Research

Research at Wills Eye was initiated almost singlehandedly by Irving Leopold. A native of Philadelphia who trained with Francis Adler, he became involved with clinical warfare research during World War II. This led to his development of diisopropyl fluorophosphate or fluoropryl (DFP), which was first encountered and used in ophthalmology while being investigated as a chemical warfare agent. At that time, Leopold was working for the Office of Scientific Research and Development (OSRD), which had two major subdivisions: the Manhattan Project and the Committee on Medical Research (CMR). Leopold was on the OSRD and CMR, dealing with ocular gas casualties.

DFP was interesting because very small concentrations in vapor form produced marked miosis, lasting much longer than any miotic action previously observed in ophthalmology. Because of this unusual finding, at the end of the war the Chemical Warfare Service requested use of this agent in two ways: for study in patients with myasthenia gravis and to determine whether it could be used in the management of glaucoma. The hope was to reduce the frequency of instillation of drops required to maintain satisfactory intraocular pressure.

Considerable animal experimentation had already been done and had proved that this was an anticholinesterase agent. Experiments such as ciliary ganglionectomy and cervical sympathectomy were performed, and these established that this was a so-called irreversible anticholinesterase agent in the eye. With repeated instillation into rabbit eyes over a period of many months, no lens opacities could be demonstrated. Leopold also studied the ability of this agent, when topically applied to the eye, to inhibit human serum cholinesterase and set about trying the drug in various types of glaucoma. Response curves were established in rabbit eyes and normal human eyes, and the effectiveness of the drug in glaucoma was established.

The drug was tried in strabismus, and the results were published shortly after the war in the *Archives of Ophthalmology*. It was proved as an effective agent for cases that were not responding to pilocarpine or epinephrine.

DFP had one significant disadvantage in solution: it had to be made up in an anhydrous peanut oil, because it tended to very rapidly lose its potency in water. For this reason, after finding this drug and utilizing it for glaucoma, Leopold was on the constant lookout for an anticholinesterase agent that would be stable in water. One was called 217AO; the other, which did not penetrate into the central nervous system, was 217MI. 217MI, later known as phospholine iodide or echothiophate iodide, was selected for use in the eye because many researchers had discovered that DFP could penetrate into the central nervous system and on occasion produced bizarre dreams.

Phospholine iodide is stable in water for reasonable periods of time. Response curves were established, and it was tried in normal human eyes after studies in experimental eyes, where it was found to be effective. At no time was the development of lens opacities or retinal detachment in experimental animals demonstrated. Human experience has shown a tendency for strong anticholinesterase agents, as well as all cholinergic agents, to produce lens opacities in glaucomatous eyes. Phospholine iodide was also found to be effective in esotropia and strabismus of the accommodative variety.

When Leopold came to the Wills Hospital after World War II as an assistant in the Warren Reese Clinic, there was no experimental research going on. The Board of Surgeons and the Board of Trustees granted permission for him to set up some areas for such research in basement rooms in which there were ventilation ducts. During that period a number of individuals worked in these facilities, including Robert Day, who is now in New York, and ex-resident Tom Dickinson. As research grants were obtained from NIH and other awarding groups, however, it became apparent that there was insufficient room to carry out the necessary work.

As a result, the Board of City Trusts obtained a dilapidated building on Brandywine Street behind the hospital for approximately $3,000 (Fig 11-1) (At that time, Mr. Ernest Trigg was the head of the Wills Committee of the Board of City Trusts.)

This building had to be refurbished, and the members of the staff of the Wills Hospital contributed toward its reconstruction (Fig 11-1). The funds raised at that time were $22,000. There was a plaque in the hall listing the contributors. In addition, various philanthropic groups in the city purchased equipment and helped to refurbish the building and to set up a research laboratory. Some of the groups that contributed were the Lions and the Vida Lodge; many private patients of staff doctors also made contributions. Purchase of some of the equipment was supported by grants from NIH, the National Council to Combat Blindness, and the National Society for Prevention of Blindness.

The three floors were outfitted. The first floor included animal quarters in the rear, operating rooms, and an electron microscope on a firm base in the front. The second floor essentially housed micro-biology and the third floor biochemistry. Individuals such as Dr. Virginia Weimer and Dr. Harry Green began to work in this department, along with a number of residents and research fellows, including Stanley Capper, a physiologist, and H. Shapiro, Jim O-Rourke, George Spaeth, Arthur Calnan, and L. K. Sarin.

After this laboratory had been used for a reasonable period, it once again became apparent that there was insufficient space, although the labs were doing creditable work that was calling attention to experimental studies at the Wills Eye Hospital.

Drs. Virginia Weimer and Harry Green were doing studies on corticosteroid penetration, lens metabolism, wound healing, and the factors that influence drug penetration. Harry Green and his staff were working on acetazolamide and its mechanism of action. Michael Kazurowski was beginning his anatomical studies. Frank Furguiele did a fellowship on antibiotic penetration, and Adolph Vogel started his oncologic drug toxicity and choroidal circulation studies. Enrique Wudka extended these and worked on scleral resections.

At this point, the Board of City Trusts was sufficiently impressed so that when the Ford Foundation funds were released to hospitals throughout the United States, the Board of City Trusts decided to use the funds for the construction of a new research laboratory.

With the architectural help of Vincent Kling, the new research

Fig 11-1. The first research building before, during, and after renovation.

Fig 11-1. (*continued*).

laboratories were built; use of the initial research building also continued, because this space was still needed (Fig 11-2 through 11-4).

By this time, Winston Barber and Ted Sery had joined the group, and the laboratory continued to be productive in many areas. Studies continued on penetration of antibiotics, corticosteroids, wound healing, herpes, and tumor growth. Additional hardworking research fellows include Florian Maylath, Fikret Mutlu, Satya Dev Paul, Paul Carmichael, and S. Kurose.

Today Wills research includes NIH grants to study diabetic

New Laboratory Dedicated at Wills Hospital

By JOSEPH F. NOLAN
Inquirer Medical Editor

City and State officials took part yesterday in the dedication of the new $65,000 laboratory and department of research of the Wills Eye Hospital, which is located on Brandywine st. near 16th, directly in the rear of the hospital.

The new research laboratory was completed by funds from various organizations and from the Federal Government under the Hill-Burton Hospital Construction Act, which provided $13,000 toward the building.

Members of various Lions Clubs

Fig 11-2. Dedication of a second research building.

The Board of Directors of City Trusts

requests the honor of your presence

at the ceremony attending the

Dedication

of the

Department of Research Laboratories

at

Wills Eye Hospital

Tuesday, the seventh of October

nineteen hundred and fifty-two

two o'clock

Sixteenth and Spring Garden Streets

Fig 11-2. (*continued*).

Program

Dedication of

NEW RESEARCH LABORATORY OF WILLS EYE HOSPITAL

Sunday, September 20, 1959 at 1 P.M.

Opening Remarks
MR. J. GRIFFITH BOARDMAN, *Chairman*
Committee on Research
Board of Directors of City Trusts

Invocation
REV. JOHN C. MCGLADE, C.S.SP., *Director*
St. Joseph's House for Boys

Welcome to Wills Eye Hospital
MR. SAMUEL H. DAROFF, *President*
Board of Directors of City Trusts

Greetings from the Medical Staff
WILFRED E. FRY, M.D., *President*
Board of Attending Surgeons
Wills Eye Hospital

Comment
MR. JOHN A. DIEMAND, *Former President*
Board of Directors of City Trusts

Remarks
EDWIN B. DUNPHY, M.D., *Henry Willard Williams Professor of Ophthalmology, Harvard Medical School and Chief of Ophthalmology, Massachusetts Eye and Ear Infirmary*

A. E. MAUMENEE, M.D., *William Holland Wilmer Professor of Ophthalmology and Director of Department of Ophthalmology, Johns Hopkins University School of Medicine*

IRVING H. LEOPOLD, M.D., *Director of Research, Wills Eye Hospital and Professor of Ophthalmology, Graduate School of Medicine, University of Pennsylvania*

Address
His Excellency—DAVID L. LAWRENCE, *Governor*
of the Commonwealth of Pennsylvania

Benediction
REV. JERRY E. CARPENTER, *Director*
Institutional Chaplaincy
Episcopal Community Services

Tour of New Research Laboratory

Fig 11-2. (*continued*).

Fig 11-3. Designed by Vincent Kling, the new research building was next door to the original one.

Fig 11-4. Dedication ceremonies October 7, 1952. (Left to right, Dr. Sam McPherson, Dr. Irving Leopold, Dr. Edwin Dunphy of the Massachusetts Eye and Ear Infirmary, and Dr. Parker Heath.

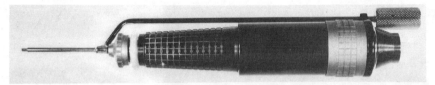

Fig 11-5. Suction infusion tissue extractor (SITE) for vitrectomy surgery.

retinopathy, corneal diseases, glaucoma, immunology, intraocular tumors, and vitreoretinal diseases, in addition to continuation of basic research activities. As a result, Wills at present is in every sense of the word a tertiary eye care center. It is renowned for the diagnosis and management of ocular tumors and is credited with the development of the suction infusion tissue extractor (SITE) for vitreous surgery (Fig 11-5).

Chapter 12

Wills Eye Hospital: 1980

As surgical techniques grew complex, it became apparent to officials of Wills Eye Hospital that it would be prudent for their hospital to be affiliated with a medical school. Each could then share the other's facilities, as well as their expertise. Therefore, on July 20, 1972, an agreement was signed between the Board of City Trusts and Thomas Jefferson University for such a merger. Both institutions felt that the affiliation would eliminate costly duplication of services, such as x-ray equipment, pharmaceutical facilities, and the library. In addition, Jefferson's emergency department would be shared with Wills Eye Hospital in order to provide continuous, 24-hour service.

This merger, however, did not change the fact that both institutions were separate and independent. It did mean that the new Wills Eye Hospital would be located near its partner school in an up-to-date modern facility. Therefore, the site on the southwest corner of Ninth and Walnut Streets was selected (Fig 12-1).

Future plans include eventual integration of the staffs and facilities of the new institution. In the interim, Wills Eye will encourage all Jefferson interns, residents, and fellows to take full advantage of a wide range of ophthalmology programs. The two institutions will now train orthoptists, ocularists, and other paramedicals together. Jefferson in turn will offer its general hospital expertise to Wills Eye patients requiring neurologic, vascular, general medical, and metabolic services.

It is quite clear that the new hospital could not have been accomplished without the support of the Board of City Trusts and the

Work slated on new home for Wills Eye Hospital

By Robert Fensterer
Inquirer Staff Writer

The Philadelphia hospital with a reputation as a world leader in eye treatment is moving to a larger building.

Wills Eye Hospital, located since 1932 in a six-story building at 16th and Spring Garden Streets, will break ground this winter for a $25 million building at Ninth and Walnut Streets, next to the Jefferson University campus. January 1980 is the target date for moving.

The City Planning Commission has approved the plans and the Hospitals Authority of Philadelphia has agreed to float a $22 million municipal bond issue.

The $3 million difference will be raised through contributions or by same number of beds as the old, as well as the same eye therapy equipment.

Staff doctors at Wills are pleased that they will be affiliated with the university next door.

"That means," said Dr. George L. Spaeth, head of the glaucoma clinic, "that when I examine a patient and find he has other ailments I will no longer have to send him all over town to other specialists. I will have all the specialists I need right here on the same campus."

A joint purchasing arrangement, Joseph said, will keep operating costs down.

The coming move reminded Dr. Spaeth of 1960, when he began his residency at Wills. Then, all patients were treated in three huge general clinics and all doctors saw all types of patients.

"It was fantastic training," he said. "But it was old-fashioned medicine. It hadn't changed since 1832.

That was the year that trustees of the James Wills estate interpreted the phrase in his will, "care for the indigent blind," to mean a hospital dedicated to the treatment of eye diseases.

A building on the southeast corner of Logan Square housed the hospital for exactly 100 years. In 1932, the Spring Garden building was opened.

Fig 12-1. Wills plans to move to 9th and Walnut Streets.

even-handed leadership of the present ophthalmologist-in-chief, Thomas Duane (Fig 12-2). Working with him and also sharing a major role in the accomplishment of our new facility is the administrator, Mr. David Joseph.

The new hospital is an eight-story building with 225,000 square feet of floor space (Fig 12-3); this is considerably more than Spring Garden Street's 140,000 square feet. The number of beds, however, remains at 120. The additional space will allow continued expansion of the outpatient, research, and education areas. General ophthalmology will continue, and the same subspecialty clinics in retina, cornea, glaucoma, oculoplastics, neuroophthalmology, uveitis and pediatric ophthalmology will be available.

In addition to its own strong staff, Wills has supplied leaders to other institutions as well. Its graduates are affiliated with teaching departments in Atlanta, Florida, Pittsburgh, Texas, and New York, and one

98

of its most illustrious alumni, William R. Green, is professor of ophthalmology and associate professor of pathology at the Johns Hopkins School of Medicine and director of the Eye Pathology Laboratory at the Wilmer Institute (Fig 12-4).

The Wills staff has depth in every department and is clinically and academically oriented. Members on all services have international reputations in their particular specialty. Many have authored or edited significant books, not the least of which is Duane's *Textbook of Ophthalmology*, the best textbook of general ophthalmology available today. They serve on important committees, as officers in national societies, and on the editorial boards of important journals. For over 150 years Wills has been in the forefront of ophthalmology. Now, it looks confidently to the 1980s and beyond.

Fig 12-2. Our ophthalmologist-in-chief, Thomas D. Duane.

Fig 12-3. From a hole in the ground to near completion.

Fig 12-3. (*continued*).

Fig 12-4. Alumnus William Richard Green.

The Board of City Trusts

William P. Cairo
Joseph A. Daroff
Louis J. Esposito
Harry R. Halloran
Melvin C. Howell
Herbert J. Hutton
Edward J. Kane
Max M. Leon
William A. Meehan
Donald C. Reubel
Isadore A. Shrager
Kate Skale

Ruth Armour, Secretary
Gaffney and Gaffney, Solicitors

Ex-Officio Members:

The Mayor of the City of Philadelphia

The President of City Council

The Wills Eye Hospital Advisory Council

Barr E. Asplundh
Richard C. Bond
Edward C. Driscoll
Thomas D. Duane, M.D., Ex-Officio
Mrs. Richard Ellis
Louis J. Esposito
Harry R. Halloran
Maurice Heckscher
David S. Joseph, Ex-Officio
Martin Keenan
Horace L. Kephart
W. Thacher Longstreth
Robert D. Mulberger, M.D.
John C. Pemberton
George M. Ross
John M. Seabrook
William S. Tasman, M.D.

The Wills Eye Hospital Staff

Thomas D. Duane, M.D.
Ophthalmologist-in-Chief

CORNEA SERVICE

Attending Surgeon

P. R. Laibson

Consultants

O.R. Kline, Jr.
R.D. Mulberger
P.G. Spaeth

Associate Surgeon

J.J. Arentsen

Senior Assistant Surgeon

H.T. Dodds
M.A. Naidoff
P.R. Tolat

Assistant Surgeon

D.R. Ehrlich

GENERAL RECEIVING

Attending Surgeon

O. Belmont
M.J. Dougherty
R.A. Ellis
T.N. Hamdi

O.R. Kline, Jr.
R.D. Mulberger
P.G. Spaeth

Consultants

J.W. Hallett
P.J. Kennedy

Associate Surgeon

E.H. Bedrossian
T. Behrendt
H.W. Forster, Jr.
E. A. Jaeger
W. Kamerling
J. Katz
E.U. Keates

K.I. Michaile
F.O. Nagle, Jr.
P.V. Palena
C.G. Steinmetz III
F.P. Sutliff
A. Weiner

Senior Assistant Surgeon

R.E. Adams
C.M. Alexander
W.M. Bryant
R.W. Connor
D.G. Durham
S.H. Franklin
B.D. Galman
H.P. Koller
R.M. Lubowitz

A.C. Martinez
A.P. Murray
M.A. Naidoff
D.F. Perkins
L.W. Schwartz
J. Spina, Jr.
L.X. Viggiano
A.W. Vogel

Assistant Surgeon

M.H. Balistocky
E.F. Becker
R.W. Bell
E.J. Cannon
J.J. Coyle
E.A. Deglin
A.R. Forman
H.T. Friebel
J.G. Friedberg
F. Frisch, Jr.
W.S. Gan
I.S. Hneleski
P. Horowitz
B.P. Houser, Jr.
R.C. Jalbuena
J.B. Jeffers
T.S. Johnston
J. Kalin
W. Kustrup
G.S. Levin
J.S. Levin

S.B. Lichtenstein
C.A. Michon
R.V. Miller
C.L. Mineo
H.J. Nevyas
W.F. Rath
M.W. Richman
C.R. Rickards
R.S. Sando
P.J. Savino
H.B. Schwandt
P.D. Shawaluk
D.J. Smith
A.M. Spiegelman
G.W. Stubbs
L.H. Sweterlitsch, Jr.
J.C. Toland
A.F. Traupman
N. Vacharat
H.K. Yang

Clinical Assistant

H.E. Buch
T. Buckner
T.O. Burkholder
F.L. Dankmyer
P.H. Geetter
E.W. Gerner
D.S. Hyman
A.M. Interdonato
M.L. Kay
S. Kessler
J.B. Light
T.L. Manzo
J.I. Markoff

D.D. Mecca
J.F. Morrison
J.Y. Nevyas
D.S.C. Pao
P.J. Racciato
P. Remer
R.S. Rowley
L.S. Schaffzin
F.F. Spechler
J.C. Tassini
R.L. Tax
M.A. Wolf
H.K. Yang

GLAUCOMA SERVICE

Attending Surgeon

G.L. Spaeth

Consultants

H.D. Barnshaw

Associate Surgeon

K.W. Benjamin
A.K. Chan
E. Sivalingam

Senior Assistant Surgeon

L.W. Schwartz
H.A. Scimeca

Assistant Surgeon

M.E. Starrels
R.P. Wilson

Clinical Assistant

R.S. Sando

NEUROOPHTHALMOLOGY

Attending Surgeon

N.J. Schatz

Consultants

B.J. Alpers
N.S. Schlezinger

Associate Surgeon

P.J. Savino
W.H. Whiteley

Clinical Assistant

W.H. Cobbs

OCULOPLASTICS

Attending Surgeon

G.M. Shannon

Consultants

R.D. Mulberger
P.G. Spaeth

Associate Surgeon

J.C. Flanagan
J.J. Siliquini

Senior Assistant Surgeon

J.H. Negrey, Jr.

Assistant Surgeon

C.L. Mineo
R.H. White, Jr.
J.G. Yassin

PEDIATRIC OPHTHALMOLOGY

Attending Surgeon

J.H. Calhoun
D.R. Manley

Consultants

R.D. Harley

Associate Surgeon

E.H. Bedrossian

Appendices

Senior Assistant Surgeon

H.P. Koller

Clinical Assistant

B.D. Altman

RETINA SERVICE

Attending Surgeon

W.H. Annesley, Jr.
L.K. Sarin
W.S. Tasman

Consultants

P.R. McDonald
M.J. Mastrangelo

Associate Surgeon

W.E. Benson
P.L. Carmichael
J.L. Federman

R.E. Goldberg
A.C. Lucier

Senior Assistant Surgeon

A.W. Zimmerman

Assistant Surgeon

L.E. Magargal

Clinical Assistant

R.C. Lanning

ONCOLOGY

Attending Surgeon

J.A. Shields

PATHOLOGY SERVICE

Attending Surgeon

V.B. Bernardino, Jr.

Assistant Ophthalmic Pathologist

J.J. Arentsen
J.L. Federman
R.M. Lubowitz

N. Romayanando
J.A. Shields

Consultant, Ophthalmic Pathologist

W.H. Clark, Jr.
G.H. Kurz
J.S. McGavic

C.G. Steinmetz III
A.S. Patchefsky

CONSULTING SURGEONS

Francis H. Adler
Harold D. Barnshaw
Albert F. Cleveland
Glen G. Gibson
Joseph W. Hallett
Robison D. Harley
William T. Hunt, Jr.
Patrick J. Kennedy
Irving H. Leopold
P. Robb McDonald
Sidney G. Radbill
Warren S. Reese
Joseph Waldman

CONSULTING OPHTHALMOLOGISTS

Solomon S. Brav
Edward C. Jennings
Max D. Kasser
Henry J. Kohler
Edward I. Lipsius

Charles A. Rankin
Charles J. Rife
William P. Robinson
E. Pierce Shope
Joseph M. Tillman
Robert W. Traganza
Sidney Weiss
Michael I. Wolkowicz

CONSULTING PHYSICIAN

Harold A. Hanno

CONSULTING ASSOCIATE PHYSICIANS

Nathan S. Schlezinger
Joseph H. Zeigerman

COURTESY STAFF

Ralph S. Milner

HONORARY STAFF

Guy H. Chan
Lois J. Martyn

ANCILLARY SERVICES

Anesthesiology

John J. Leahy *Director*
Margaret M. Libonati *Anesthesiologist*
Antonio C. Ano *Assistant Anesthesiologist*
Leonardo N. Ventura *Assistant Anesthesiologist*
Samuel Blank *Consulting Anesthesiologist*

Dermatology and Syphilology

Herbert A. Luscombe   *Director*

General Surgery

Charles C. Wolferth, Jr.   *Consultant*

Gynecology

Alan Rubin   *Director*

Internal Medicine

John H. Martin   *Consultant*
Guy E. McElwain   *Consultant*
Alan G. Adler   *Consultant*
Charles M. Thompson   *Medical Director of Employee Health*

Neurosurgery

William H. Whiteley   *Consultant*

Orthopedic Surgery

Jerome M. Cotler   *Consultant*

Otolaryngology

Diran O. Mikaelian   *Director*
Martin T. Brennan   *Consultant, Otolaryngology*
Emilio A. Roncace   *Consultant, Ortorhinolaryngology*

Pediatrics

Robert L. Brent   *Consultant*
Gary C. Carpenter   *Consultant*
Gary A. Emmett   *Consultant*

Gerald A. Fendrick   *Consultant*
Harry D. Getz   *Consultant*
Arturo R. Hervada   *Consultant*
Jeanette C. Mason   *Consultant*
Stephen J. McGeady   *Consultant*
Sylvester L. Mobley   *Consultant*
Floyd T. Nasuti   *Consultant*
Irving J. Olshin   *Consultant*
Theodore S. Tapper   *Consultant*
Jeffrey C. Weiss   *Consultant*

Roentgenology

Armand L. Bernabei   *Consultant*
Robert D. Hochberg   *Consultant*
Ernesto E. Lucena   *Consultant*

Urology

P. Kenneth Brownstein   *Consultant*

Resident Surgeons

1839	John Neill	1867	John C. Campbell
1841	Samuel L. Hollingsworth	1867	Elliott Richardson
1842	George N. Burwell	1868	Marshall Paul
1843	John Owen	1868	George Roberts
1844	Robert O. Norris	1869	J.C. Wilson
1845	Robert Newton	1869	Morris Longsworth
1846	Daniel G. Heylman	1870	William C. Cox
1847	Alfred M. Slocum	1871	N.G. Macomber
1848	Irene A. Young	1872	E.Y. Burroughs
1849	Henry G. Graham	1872	H.D. Bendt
1850	Archibald J. McIntyre	1873	J.A. Lippincott
1851	James S. Green	1874	A. Stockman
1852	Theophilus Parvin	1875	Frank Fisher
1853	Norval W. Littell	1876	W.M. Mastyn
1854	John C. Homan	1876	G.W. Bligler
1855	John C. Kitchen	1877	W.C. Henderson
1856	Isaac N. Kerlin	1878	J.P. Perkins
1856	T. George Morton	1879	J.J. Owens
1857	George C. Harlan	1880	J.H. Carrier
1858	Edward Livezey	1881	B.L. Millikin
1859	Charles C. Lee	1882	George R. Rohrer
1860	Charles E. Hackley	1883	Charles W. Kollock
1861	William Savery	1884	George T. Lewis
1862	Joseph G. Richardson	1885	Henry Sykes
1862	Thomas Wister	1886	C.A. Woodnut
1863	Charles T. Palmer	1887	S. Lewis Beigler
1865	Charles H. Thomas	1889	Joseph Otto
1866	William W. McClure	1890	M.W. Zimmerman

1891	Paul J. Pontius	1914	J.W. Thompson
1892	E.C. Ellett	1915	Otis J. Simonds
1892	Walter R. Parker	1915	Harry V. Judge
1893	Paul Guilford	1916	Frederick A. Schlanger
1893	A.S. Wilson	1916	Joseph V. Connole
1894	G.E. Curry	1917	Warren S. Reese
1894	Burton Chance	1917	William S. Holzer
1895	D.E. Esterly	1918	R.S. Pendexter
1896	James C. Bloomfield	1918	O.H. Yereman
1896	Edward R. Roderick	1919	Earnest L. Posey
1897	Clinton J. Kistler	1919	Orea J. Parks
1897	Edmund D. Shortlidge	1920	Lee W. Hughes
1898	Frank A. Ford	1920	Joseph E. Beideman
1898	Albert C. Snell	1921	Cecil S. O'Brien
		1921	Cecil P. Clark
1901	Harold G. Goldberg	1922	Charles A. Young
1902	Homer J. Rhode	1922	Ivan J. Koenig
1902	W. L. Carrol	1923	Frank C. Smith
1903	John R. Taylor	1923	Walter H. Funk
1903	Robert I. Bullard	1924	Howard F. Hill
1904	James A. Kearney	1924	Thurber LeWin
1904	Owen M. Deems	1924	John S. Plumer
1905	William G. Schlindwein	1924	Hayward J. Blackmon
1905	J. Clyde Markel	1925	George J. Dublin
1906	Samuel B. Hayes	1926	Wilfred T. Gratton
1906	G.A. Briggs	1926	Leo W. Funk
1907	J. Milton Griscom	1926	James S. Shipman
1907	Carl Boardman	1926	Maurice E. Marcove
1907	Carl Boardman	1927	Wilfred E. Muldoon
1908	Charles W. Jennings	1927	Walter C. Mott
1908	Emory Hill	1927	Lewis P. Glover
1909	Frank E. Detling	1928	William J. Burdshaw
1909	Nelson S. Weinberger	1928	Pierre G. Jenkins
1910	Thomas H. Cates	1928	James H. Delaney
1910	John A. Kenney	1929	Noel T. Simmonds
1912	J.B. Moore	1929	Thomas G. McLellan
1912	C.M. Buckner	1929	I. Jenkins Mikell
1913	Samuel Marshall	1930	John B. Moore
1913	H.C. Schmitz	1930	William C. Ostrom
1914	Paul H. Kleinhans	1930	Raymond N. Burke
1914	W.E. Carson	1930	Stacy C. Howell

1931	Ethelburt B. Fairbanks	1940	Charles Ruggeri
1931	James M. Baird	1940	Ned Schwartz
1931	William H.M. Thomson	1940	John W. Deichler
1931	E. Leonard Goodman	1941	Daniel J. Fisher
1932	Walter L. Forster	1941	Harold M. U'Ren
1932	Benjamin Wolpaw	1941	Charles L. O'Neill
1932	Noel S. McBride	1941	Frank T. Cultrona
1932	Louis D. Gomon	1941	Henry Abrams
1932	Carl D.F. Jensen	1942	Theodore Long
1933	E.R. Anderson	1942	Harvey C. Ennio
1933	James S. Jordan	1942	Irving L. Pavlo
1933	Ronald A. Cox	1942	Samuel J. Altman
1933	Alvin W. Howland	1942	Robert E. Shoemaker
1933	Robert E. Rohm	1942	Garland M. Johnson
1934	John M. Wotring	1943	Harry J. French
1934	James E. Wilson	1943	James B. Vaughan
1934	James J. Finegan	1943	Stanley W. Boland
1934	Samuel Phillips	1943	Ruth Leonard
1935	Roscoe J. Kennedy	1944	Juan A. Diaz
1935	Robert S. Minton	1944	Elbert C. Anderson
1935	Henry K. Erwin	1944	Joseph J. Morrison
1935	William D. Angle	1944	Francis X. Budd
1936	L.M. Gurley	1944	Norbert F. Albertstadt
1936	Robb McDonald	1944	Raphael Alan Fawcett
1936	Van M. Ellis	1944	Dorothy Campbell
1936	Irvin Levy	1945	August J. Podboy
1937	James V.D. Quereau	1945	Reuben G. Alexander
1937	John S. Goldcamp	1945	Harvey D. Wright
1937	Daniel B. Esterly	1945	George E. Martz
1937	Warren C. Phillips	1945	I. Harvey Plain
1938	John L. Matthews	1945	Thomas C. Naugle
1938	Samuel Wenger	1945	Peter Sykowski
1938	Carl A. Holfer	1946	W. Paxson Chalfant
1938	James M. O'Brien	1946	H. Gordon Anderson
1938	Clyde H. Jacobs	1946	Marvin N. Lymberis
1939	Carl F. Breisacher	1946	Edwin R. Irgens
1939	Kenneth L. Roper	1946	Paul E. McFarland
1939	Walter J. Romejko	1946	Albert J. Cleveland
1939	E. Franklin Carl	1946	Levon K. Garron
1940	Arthur S. Clay	1946	Frederick C. Kohlmeyer
1940	Norbert W. Humpage	1946	Octavius Capriotti

1946	Russell N. Brown	1953	Philip G. Spaeth
1947	Robert E. Duprey	1953	John T. Gocke
1947	Emile M. Ravdin	1953	Robert E. Lee Shumate
1947	John L. Goff	1953	William M. McCarthy
1947	Robert A. Brown	1954	Irwin S. Turner
1947	Ernest H. Heydt	1956	Stanley A. Capper
1947	William L. Hoon	1956	Enrique Wudka
1947	Turgut Hamdi	1956	Khalida Naib
1947	Joseph W. Taylor, Jr.	1956	Arthur Labelle
1948	James H. Parker	1956	Gerard M. Shannon
1948	Isadore Eisenberg	1957	Emma C. Muller
1948	William E. Pickett	1957	Arthur F. Calnan
1948	James F. Ward	1957	Walter A. Fairfax
1948	George E. Hobach	1957	Howard K. Clough
1948	John P. Hobach	1957	Leonard Apt
1948	Merrill H. Wollmington	1957	Robert E. Maynard
1948	Edward C. Walston	1957	Harry W. Camp
1949	Clemens Kirchgeorg	1957	Francis J. Kanofsky
1949	James E. Purnell	1958	Oswald C.C. De Melo
1949	Oram R. Kline	1958	Reginald J. Raban
1949	Alan J. Rosenberg	1958	Edward C. Shrader
1949	Arthur H. Keeney	1958	William L. Eubanks
1949	Albert E. Leggett, Jr.	1958	Kenneth I. Michaile
1950	Thomas T. Dickinson	1958	Jerome Dersh
1950	Paul Kahn, Jr.	1958	Robert C. Lee
1950	Albert W. McCally	1958	Samuel W. Knisely
1950	Richard H. Seely	1959	Milton Boniuk
1950	Owen Belmont	1959	E.R. Gonzalez Jinnenez
1951	Karl M. Aijian	1959	Ralph S. Hamilton*
1951	Charles G. Steinmetz III	1959	Myron A. Portenar
1951	William H. Annesley	1959	Arnold G. Kushner
1951	Robert Anthony	1959	Alex D. MacAskill
1951	Cyril M. Luce	1959	Joseph Amdur
1951	Florian R. Maylath	1960	Arnold L. Rose
1952	Mila J. Ashodian	1960	Romeo V. Fajardo
1952	James F. O'Rourke	1960	William Kamerling
1952	Emery E. Royce	1960	Malvin J. Dougherty
1953	Thomas J. McKenna	1960	Jerome A. Montana*
1953	William K. Wheatly	1960	Lloyd W. Bailey
1953	Robert E. Murto	1960	Charles Kelman
1953	Paul A. Gold	1961	John J. Martin

1961	David M. Warner		1967	Michael D. Cefaratti
1961	Edwin U. Keates		1967	William J. Kustrup
1961	Ernest H. Coleman		1967	Joseph C. Flanagan
1961	Clay W. Evatt		1967	David Meyer
1961	William S. Tasman*		1967	Barbara Mitchell
1961	Daniel I. Weiss		1967	P. Kenneth Nase
1962	Jonathan A. Holloway*		1967	Hunter R. Stokes*
1962	Edward G. Dailey		1968	H. Thomas Dodds
1962	Robert H. Fessler		1968	Bert R. Estlow
1962	Louis X. Viggiano		1968	Barry D. Galman
1962	Arthur M. Spiegleman		1968	Kurt A. Gitter
1962	Gerald J. Chessen		1968	Richard D. Hyman*
1962	Philip L. Levy		1968	Kenneth R. Jaegers
1963	George L. Spaeth*		1968	David J. Singer
1963	Donald L. Praeger		1968	M. Madison Slusher
1963	Horry H. Kerrison		1969	Joseph H. Calhoun
1963	Basil Manley, Jr.		1969	James E. Copeland
1963	William R. Green		1969	Burton M. Cunin
1963	Ronald B. Vittone		1969	Ben P. Houser*
1963	Robert E. King		1969	Donald P. Lewin
1964	Raymond E. Adams*		1969	Alfred C. Lucier
1964	I. Allen Chirls		1969	Cyrus L. Mineo
1964	Thomas L. Gorman		1969	Donald F. Perkins
1964	Ralph N. Goulston		1970	William R. Griffith*
1964	Sanford D. Hecht		1970	Pierre Guibor
1964	Peter R. Laibson		1970	William K. Harris
1964	Stanley L. Spielman		1970	Martin B. Kaplan
1965	Stanley W. Boland		1970	Michael D. McManus
1965	Line Chevrette		1970	Joel Porter
1965	John J. Coyle		1970	Jerry A. Shields
1965	William F. Grant		1970	Robert H. White, Jr.
1965	Philip C. Hughes*		1970	E. Randolph Wilkerson
1965	Philip M. Levy		1970	Samuel Miller Winn
1965	Ronald L. Spielman		1971	William Alton Bohart
1966	Robert W. Connor		1971	Brenton C. Burgoyne
1966	Richard E. Goldberg		1971	Henderson J. Cleaves
1966	Donelson R. Manley*		1971	John B. Jeffers
1966	Morton W. Richman		1971	Neil M. Krosney
1966	Norman J. Fisher		1971	David H. Miller
1966	John W. Tomlinson		1971	Robert V. Miller
1966	Cyril J. Walsh		1971	Larry M. Piebenga

119

1971	Robert E. Searle	1974	Harold I.R. Sawelson
1971	Robert L. Shindler	1974	Edward Mark Sorr
1971	Richard W. Sonntag*	1974	William V. Tillery
1971	Bruce C. Taylor	1975	Joshua N. Babad
1971	John H. Weaver	1975	Bernard Heersink
1971	James E. Wilson, Jr.	1975	James E. Heeter
1972	Robert L. Alan	1975	Douglas A. MacLeod
1972	Samuel Sunday Amoni	1975	David B. Mallory
1972	Ann E. Barker	1975	Bernard E. Patty
1972	William Alden Blank	1975	John D. Polansky
1972	Theodore Buckner	1975	John J. Purcell*
1972	J. Sidney Cotner	1975	Michael L. Steiner
1972	Thomas F. Drake	1975	Sanford Ullman
1972	Eyck W. Fintelmann	1976	Andrew Davidson
1972	Patrick D. Moore	1976	Daniel M. Kane
1972	William N. Offutt	1976	Philip H. McKinley*
1972	Hyman William Ross	1976	Jerry W. Maida
1972	Vincent A. Sanderson	1976	James L. Mims
1972	Jonathan D. Trobe*	1976	Paul R. Mitchell
1972	Ira Gary Weiner	1976	D. Parker Stokes
1973	Bruce R. Berg	1976	Richard T. Tax
1973	Stephen G. Cook	1976	Stephen W. Wong
1973	Joseph J. DeVenuto	1977	Robert S. Baxter
1973	Ido Egerer	1977	Craig H. Douglas*
1973	Neil H. Joseph	1977	Jorge A. Godinez
1973	Stephen M. Moehlman	1977	Marnix Heersink
1973	Moira B. Murphy	1977	Alan E. Irwin
1973	Louis W. Schwartz	1977	Joseph B. Michelson
1973	J.H. Stokes, Jr.	1977	Ronald R. Reed
1973	John R. Trittschuh	1977	Paul Remer
1973	George Waring	1977	Ralph S. Sando
1973	Edward J. Zobian*	1977	David J. Smith
1973	John F. Moretti	1977	James Tassini
1974	G.R. Barvinchak	1978	Thomas O. Burkholder
1974	James B. Carty*	1978	Edward C. Clark
1974	Richard A. Getnick	1978	Steven N. Cohen
1974	R.H. Goodwin, Jr.	1978	Cono M. Grasso
1974	William J. Jordan	1978	Stephen B. Lichtenstein*
1974	Charles E. Letocha	1978	Joseph I. Markoff
1974	John N. Negrey	1978	Peter J. Racciato
1974	Robert H. Nicholson	1978	Leon L. Remis

1978	Richard S. Rowley
1978	Robert F. Stephens
1978	Richard P. Wilson
1979	Dennis Arinella
1979	Susan Benes
1979	Gary Brown*
1979	Elisabeth Cohen
1979	David Hyman
1979	W. Reed Kinderman
1979	Thomas Manzo
1979	Richard Marcello
1979	Joseph Morrison
1979	David Randell
1979	Robert Sergott
1980	Alexander Aimette
1980	Frances Barton
1980	Jonathan Belmont
1980	Geoffrey Broocker
1980	Stephen Felton
1980	Robert Folberg
1980	Andrew Levin
1980	Richard Parrish*
1980	Paul Pender

1980	Mark Ruchman
1980	Joseph Scuderi
1981	Dominick Benedetto
1981	Charles Castoro
1981	William Degenhart
1981	George Fava
1981	Gregory Gensheimer
1981	William Martin
1981	Elizabeth Miller
1981	John Rizzo
1981	Michael Zamore
1981	Robert Behar
1981	James Dickson
1981	William Kiser
1981	Don Koepsell
1981	Edward McCarthy
1981	Kenneth Moffat
1981	Mary Stefanyszyn
1981	Douglas Symes
1981	Martin Wax
1981	Michael Wong

*Chief resident.

Attending Surgeons

1834–1852	Isaac Parrish	1897–1900	John W. Croskey
1834–1864	Squier Littell	1898–1924	Peter N.K. Schwenk
1834–1854	Isaac Hays	1901–1924	McCluney Radcliffe
1834–1849	George Fox	1902–1916	S. Lewis Ziegler
1849–1852	John Neill	1901–1928	William Zentmayer
1852–1859	Edward Hartshorne	1902–1919	William C. Posey
1852–1857	Fitzwilliam Hunt	1907–1932	Paul J. Pontius
1854–1861	Addinell Hewson	1911–1919	William M. Sweet
1857–1864	William Hunt	1916–1933	Burton Chance
1859–1874	Thomas G. Morton	1917–1943	J. Milton Griscom
1863–1893	A. Douglass Hall	1919–1949	Frank C. Parker
1861–1901	George C. Harlan	1919–1924	Thomas B. Holloway
1864–1869	D. Hayes Agnew	1924–1938	B.F. Baer, Jr.
1864–1872	Richard J. Levis	1924–1941	Thomas A. O'Brien
1872–1895	H. Ernest Goodman	1924–1939	Leighton F. Appleman
1872–1873	Ezra Dyer	1933–1937	Francis H. Adler
1872–1897	Peter D. Keyser	1937–1952	Louis Lehrfeld
1872–1907	William W. McClure	1939–1957	Warren S. Reese
1872–1901	William F. Norris	1939–1961	Carroll R. Mullen
1872–1902	William Thompson	1939–1966	James S. Shipman
1872–1890	George Strawbridge	1939–1960	Edmund B. Spaeth
1877–1890	Henry S. Schell	1939–1953	William J. Harrison
1890–1911	Charles A. Oliver	1939–1960	Isaac S. Tassman
1890–1916	Frank Fisher	1943–1967	Wilfred E. Fry
1890–1917	Samuel E. Risley	1949–1971	P. Robb McDonald
1890–1898	Edward Jackson	1952–1964	Irving H. Leopold
1893–1914	Conrad Berens	1953–1972	Patrick J. Kennedy

1957–1958	Edward J. Donnelly	1973–	Peter R. Laibson
1958–	Robert D. Mulberger	1973–	George L. Spaeth
1960–1968	William E. Krewson III	1973–	Philip G. Spaeth
1960–1978	Joseph Hallett	1973–	William Tasman
1966–1972	Harold D. Barnshaw	1974–	Lov K. Sarin
1967–1973	Bernard C. Gettes	1976–	Turgut N. Hamdi
1967–1976	Robison D. Harley	1976–	Donelson R. Manley
1970–	Gerard M. Shannon	1978–	Joseph H. Calhoun
1971–	William H. Annesley Jr.	1979–	Malvin J. Dougherty
1972–1976	Albert F. Cleveland	1979–	Owen Belmont
1972–	Oram H. Kline	1979–	Richard Ellis

Postgraduate Fellows

RETINA SERVICE

1962 Lov K. Sarin	1974 David S.C. Pao
1964 Vincente De la Paz	1974 Joseph J. Timmes
1964 Herman Hunter	1974 John R. Trittschuh
1965 Sheldon P. Braverman	1975 Robert L. Lewandowski
1965 Stephen F. Elgin	1975 Carol G. Reinert
1965 A. Raymond Pilkerton	1975 Edward M. Sorr
1966 Hugh L. Morris	1975 Richard L. Winslow
1967 Guilherme Ortolan, Jr.	1976 Edward A. Deglin
1967 Albert Zimmermann	1976 Brian Leonard
1968 William S. Gilbert	1976 Larry E. Magargal
1968 David Meyer	1976 Harold Weiss
1968 Myron Yanoff	1977 David S. Boyer
1969 Richard E. Goldberg	1977 Christopher L.B. Canny
1969 Joseph Patti	1977 Stephen W. Wong
1970 Donald P. LeWin	1978 Jorge Godinez
1970 Alfred C. Lucier	1978 Leonard Joffe
1970 Peter V. Palena	1978 Richard Lanning
1971 Stanley Carson	1978 Joseph Michelson
1971 Jay L. Federman	1978 Thomas R. Pheasant
1971 Donald E. Roy	1979 Garry D. Grant
1972 Ken R. Jaegers	1979 George E. Miller
1972 Jerry A. Shields	1979 I. Richard Ombres
1972 Bruce C. Taylor	1979 Raymond E. Townsend
1972 Anthony Ramos-Umpierre	1980 James Augsburger
1973 Ira B. Fuller III	1980 Santiago Perez
1973 Hyman William Ross	1980 Robert Stephens
1973 Reid F. Schindler	1981 Gary Brown
1973 Alvin Weiner	1981 David Fischer
1974 Joseph J. DeVenuto	1981 Jeff Shakin

CORNEA SERVICE

1963	Tadeu Cvintal	1974	Neil H. Joseph
1967	Guilherme Ortolan, Jr.	1975	Jack Kabak
1968	Shashi Dhiri	1975	Juan J. Arentsen
1969	Jose T. Oconer	1976	George W. Stubbs
1969	Emauel Tanne	1976	Aisha Simje
1969	Jack Wolper	1977	Richard A. Eiferman
1970	Wendell E. Willis	1977	Walter D. Mazzanti
1970	H. Thomas Dodds	1978	James S. Allen
1971	Pratima Tolat	1978	Michael Ference III
1972	Larry Piebenga	1978	Rollande Michaud
1973	Jonathan T. Trobe	1979	Barton L. Halpern
1974	Jay H. Krachmer	1979	Irving M. Raber
1974	George O. Waring		

GLAUCOMA SERVICE

1973	M. Ahmad	1978	Nirmal Kanal
1974	R. Daniel	1978	Ralph Sando
1975	Antonio Montalbo	1979	Richard Wilson
1975	Nibondh Vacharat	1979	Suzanne Li
1976	Roger Hitchings	1979	Tharmalingam Sivendran
1977	Kinari Bakshi	1980	William Whalen
1977	Carlos Figueredo	1980	Lawrence Hurvitz
1977	Julius Satish		

NEURO-OPHTHALMOLOGY

1977	Tulay Kansu	1978	Walter Cobbs
1977	Robert Osher	1980	Susan Benes

OCULOPLASTIC SERVICE

1969	Emanuel Tanne	1973	Herbert S. Greenwald, Jr.
1970	John G. Yassin	1974	Jean-Claude Pilet
1971	Robert H. White, Jr.	1974	Jose Carlos Zenha
1971	Ignatius S. Hneleski, Jr.	1974	German S. Mendez

1975	Christine Zolli	1977	David H. Saunders
1975	John N. Negrey	1978	Ernst Nicolitz
1976	Gerald C.R. Cullen	1979	Daniel L. McLachlan
1976	Rutheva Dizon	1979	Gary L. Aguilar

PEDIATRIC OPHTHALMOLOGY SERVICE

Brian Altman
Epaminondas Branco-Neto
Miles Burke
Joseph Calhoun
Sidney Carter
James Carty
Anthony Caputo
Craig Douglas
Joao Franco
Jeffrey Hess
John Koors
Stephen Levine

Ralph Milner
James Mims
Ernest Moody
Pamela Ombres
Louis Oms
Zane Pollard
Matt Rabinowicz
Robert Sargent
Robert Schwartz
Ira Weiner
Maynard Wheeler

Nursing

Director of Patient Care

Ms. Anne Christine Tobin, B.S.N.

Assistant Director of Nursing

Mrs. Bernadette Morgan, R.N.

Administrative and Educational Supervisors

Miss Heather Boyd-Monk, R.N.
Mrs. Florence DeGeorge, R.N.
Mrs. Sharon Kuhn, R.N.

Supervisors of Nursing Units

Ms. Lisa Alexander, R.N.
Miss Maryann Hickey, R.N.
Mrs. Jane Intintolo, R.N.
Mrs. Lorraine Seifert, R.N.
Mrs. Virginia Deeney, R.N.

Administration

Administrator

David S. Joseph

Personnel

William Thorum

Public Relations

Lynn Gartland

Development

Frank Engel

Director Plant Support Services Division

Robert J. Gallos

Director Financial Services Division

Joel Davids

Director Ambulatory and Surgical Services Division

James J. Mulvihill

Bedell Lecturers

1949 Arthur Bedell
1950 Francis Heed Adler
1951 Conrad Berens
1952 Derrick Vail
1953 John H. Dunnington
            and Ellen Reagan
1954 Daniel Kirby
1955 Algernon Reese
1956 Albert Reudeman
1957 John McLean
1958 Paul Chandler
1959 Brittan Payne
1960 Peter Kronfeld
1961 Michael Hogan
1962 Frank Walsh
1963 Hans Goldmann
1964 Edmund B. Spaeth
1965 Donald Lyle
1966 A.E. Maumenee
1967 J. Barraquer
1968 Gerd Meyer-Schwickerath
1969 Harvey Thorpe
1970 David Cogan
1971 P. Robb McDonald
1972 Lorenz Zimmerman
1973 Harold G. Scheie
1974 John Mustarde
1975 Irving H. Leopold

Appendices

1976 David Shoch
1977 Charles E. Iliff
1978 Frederick Blodi
1979 Norman Jaffe
1980 Cornelius Binkhorst

Womens Committee for Wills Eye Hospital

Mrs. William H. Annesley, Jr.
Mrs. Antonio C. Año
Mrs. Carlton Asher
Mrs. Barr E. Asplundh
Mrs. James W. Bampton
Mrs. James Becker
Mrs. Kenneth Benjamin
Mrs. Milton Bennett
Mrs. Frank G. Binswanger
Mrs. Louis M. Bloom
Mrs. Robert Bolt
Mrs. Robert C. Boyd
Ms. Laila Bradley
Mrs. Solomon Brav
Miss Elizabeth M. Brown
Mrs. Chester H. Chrisler
Mrs. William Cleary
Mrs. Robert J. Coleman
Mrs. Ira L. Conkling
Mrs. Robert W. Connor
Mrs. J. Gordon Cooney
Mrs. Lee E. Cozens
Mrs. Roger J. Crossley
Mrs. Joseph M. Daly
Mrs. Sherwyn L. Davis

Mrs. Bertram C. Dedman
Mrs. Malvin J. Dougherty
Mrs. Dion Ehrlich
Mrs. Richard Ellis
Mrs. Albert R. Faber
Mrs. Arthur C. Farley
Mrs. Joseph C. Flanagan
Mrs. Wilfred E. Fry
Mrs. Remo E. Galli
Mrs. Arthur H. Gehris
Mrs. William G. Gerhard
Mrs. Walter J. Glaser
Mrs. Thomas F. Graham
Mrs. Joseph E. Griffin
Mrs. Robert Gross
Mrs. Walter S. Guggenheim
Mrs. Robert S. Hall
Mrs. Harry R. Halloran
Mrs. Turgut N. Hamdi
Mrs. Stanford Hanks
Mrs. Peter S. Hanson
Ms. Loyde Harley
Mrs. Ralph M. Harter
Mrs. Norman H. Hayes
Mrs. Robert F. Hills

Mrs. William L. Holmes
Mrs. Frederic J. Hunt, Jr.
Mrs. W. Haddon Judson
Mrs. Edward J. Kane
Mrs. Daniel M. Kane
Mrs. Charles Keller, Jr.
Mrs. Anthony J. Kennedy, Jr.
Mrs. Patrick J. Kennedy
Mrs. Ted Key
Mrs. A. Ralph Kidd
Mrs. Peter Laibson
Mrs. C. Robert Lange
Mrs. Earl K. Leedecker
Miss Esterina Lione
Mrs. Henry A. Loechner
Mrs. Alfred C. Lucier
Mrs. James F. McLoughlin
Mrs. John T. McManus
Mrs. John A. McSherry
Mrs. William S. Martin
Mrs. Cyrus Mineo
Mrs. Robert D. Mulberger
Mrs. Frank O. Nagle
Mrs. John N. Negrey
Mrs. G. Curtis Pritchard
Mrs. Charles Rankin

Mrs. Warren S. Reese
Mrs. Karl A. Roesch
Mrs. James H. Rowbotham
Mrs. G. Ellis Rumsey
Mrs. James Ryan
Mrs. Nathan Schlezinger
Mrs. Lloyd J. Schumacker
Mrs. John P. Sexton
Mrs. Gerard M. Shannon
Mrs. Michael Shekmar
Mrs. John J. Siliquini
Mrs. Joseph Skale
Mrs. Philip G. Spaeth
Miss Evelyn Stone
Mrs. Thomas P. Tanis
Mrs. William S. Tasman
Mrs. I. S. Tassman
Mrs. Elwood M. Taussig
Mrs. George Tonks
Mrs. Warner Vaughan
Mrs. Robert C. Whitmeyer
Mrs. Max T. Woodall
Mrs. Merrill H. Woolmington
Mrs. Edmund L. Zalinski
Mrs. George Zapp

Index

Index